FART PROUDLY

He that lives upon Hope,
dies Farting.

—Benjamin Franklin,
Poor Richard's Almanack, 1736

25 Dec. 2001

To Dad from Bob & Camille.
We hope you enjoy Franklin's scathing wit.

FART
PROUDLY

Writings of Benjamin Franklin
You Never Read in School

Compiled & Edited by Carl Japikse

ENTHEA PRESS
Columbus, Ohio—Atlanta, Georgia

28th Printing

Table of Contents

Introduction

*E*veryone knows Benjamin Franklin was one of the great statesmen, scientists, and philosophers of his time.

A successful printer and publisher in Philadelphia, he retired from active business in his forties and spent the rest of his life serving his community and nation. He founded the postal system in this country, served as colonial agent to Great Britain for two decades, led the protest against taxation, helped draft the Declaration of Independence, served as ambassador to France during the Revolution, organized America's first intelligence network, and helped write the Constitution that still governs this nation.

As hard as it is to believe today, however, he was even more famous in his time for his discoveries in the field of electricity—advances that made it possible for Edison, Tesla, and others to make the use of electricity practical one hundred years later. It was his immense popularity as a scientist and philosopher in France that enabled him to serve so effectively as ambassador there and gain France's aid for the colonial cause. Franklin was also an inveterate tinkerer, and is responsible for dozens of practical inventions, from bifocal lenses to the Franklin stove.

Most of these facts about Franklin's life are ones we all had to learn in school. We may have also been exposed to some of his writings—generally, his autobiography and some quotes from *Poor Richard's Almanack,* which he first published in 1733 and continued on through 1758.

But there is a side to Benjamin Franklin that we were not exposed to in school—for better or for worse, depending upon your perspective, and quite likely, the degree of your prudery. Franklin brought into this life a bawdy, scurrilous dimension of character that was all too eager to ignite the fires of controversy and, once ignited, fan the flames until they burned brightly enough to please him.

It is doubtful that Franklin thought of himself as either scandalous or roguish. He would have insisted that he just had a strong love for life and delighted in mixing things up whenever possible. He wrote and published several outright hoaxes during his career—pieces with no basis whatever in reality—just to see how quickly his readers would recognize the hoax. In many cases, most readers failed the test completely. He also loved to write satires. During his days as publisher of *The Pennsylvania Gazette* and *Poor Richard's Almanack,* most of his satire was directed at the domestic trials and tribulations of man and wife, and the foibles of society. As he became more involved in the colonial resistance to the rule of the crown, however, Franklin increasingly directed his satirical pen toward the pomposity of the English Parliament and the ministers in charge of colonial affairs.

Fart Proudly is a testament to the satirical rogue that lived peaceably inside the philosopher and statesman. But it is more than that as well; it is a loving tribute to the ideal of a free press in this country.

Once upon a time, two hundred years ago, people like Benjamin Franklin could write openly about all of the burning issues of their day. And when they wanted to express themselves pungently, because they were discussing an issue that offended their sense of smell, they were not afraid to use strong words such as "fart."

Today, "freedom of the press" is only a nostalgic idea. It is a freedom, of course, that is still guaranteed by the Constitution. But it is a freedom in name only, because the newspapers, magazines, and broadcasting stations of our great nation have lost the courage to use this freedom. They have allowed themselves to be censored, not by the government, but by the horrid specter of Social Conformity and Niceness.

It is not nice to say "fart" in public—let alone actually let one fly. It might offend someone.

It is also not nice to write about *ideas* any more, if those ideas might possibly offend someone. Whether or not the ideas contain any truth, is of no consequence; if some poor, downtrodden individual might be offended if an idea were put in print or uttered over the airwaves, then it cannot be written or stated!

This past year, the government of Iran issued a death sentence on an author who had the audacity to write a book mildly critical of fundamentalist Islam. We all shuddered and rushed to condemn this obnoxious breach of freedom of the press. And yet the media in this country routinely refuse to let ideas that might offend our own special interest groups and minorities see the light of day. They don't kill anyone, of course—they just fire them or blackball them.

The satires and songs included in this small book are not just funny pieces written two hundred years ago by someone of historical importance. Each is a direct indictment of our "free press"—a silent statement that if Franklin had written it today and tried to have it published, it would probably be censored. Not because we dislike satire, but because we dislike controversy. We do not want to offend anyone any more. We want to be Polite. We want to be Nice. Hell, we even want Safe Sex.

Benjamin Franklin was a man who loved controversy. If there wasn't any, he would stir it up. During the time he served as colonial agent, he was regarded by many people in England as "the most dangerous man in America." But do we honor this side of Franklin? Do we revere Franklin the revolutionary—or Franklin the patriarchal hero?

This is a question you can answer for yourself. Give ten of your closest friends this book as a present and ask them to read it. Two weeks later (it shouldn't take that long, but some people in modern America have forgotten how to read), ask your ten friends if they were exposed to any of these pieces in school. I will wager you that not a one of them was.

It is the side of Benjamin Franklin that Modern America wants to keep hidden.

This book, however, is determined not to let this conspiracy succeed.

If we are to preserve freedom in this country, we cannot afford to think of Benjamin Franklin as a kindly, grandfather figure who went around saying, "A penny saved is a penny earned." We must recognize that a very important part of Franklin was his love of controversy and satire. This is what made him so dangerous.

Above all, we cannot afford to think of Franklin as an antiseptic, prudish man. He was not. He was bawdy, roguish, and loved to play jokes on his friends. And when England grew oppressive, he was not afraid to rebel.

Just so, when Nature called, he farted.

And he wasn't afraid to advocate that we do the same.

FART PROUDLY

He that is conscious of
A Stink in his Breeches,
is jealous of every Wrinkle
in another's Nose.

—Benjamin Franklin,
Poor Richard's Almanack, 1751

A Letter
To A Royal Academy
1781

Editor's Note: By the time Dr. Franklin wrote this piece, he was already widely regarded as one of the premier scientists of his day, thanks mainly to his remarkable discoveries in the field of electricity. He was also widely read in all of the latest scientific theories and advances, not all of which he treated with respect. There were a number of royal academies of science, in particular, that specialized more in the trivial realms of science than the practical ones. Some of them regularly held contests in which their members were to solve complex theoretical problems, to test their skills and wit.

The best introduction to this first piece of Franklin's satire can be found in his own writings, in the form of a letter to Dr. Richard Price in 1783. We will start with the appetizer, then proceed on to the entrée.

❋ ❋ ❋

Dear Sir:

All the conversation here at present turns upon the Balloons filled with light inflammable Air....Inflammable Air puts me in mind of a little jocular paper I wrote some years since in ridicule of a prize Question given out on this side of the Water, and I enclose it for your Amusement. On second

Thoughts, as it is a mathematical Question, and perhaps I think it more trifling than it really is, and you are a Mathematician, I am afraid I have judged wrong in sending it to you. Our friend Dr. Priestley [the physicist J.B. Priestley], however, who is apt to give himself Airs, and has a kind of Right to everything his Friends Produce upon that Subject, may perhaps like to see it, and you can send it to him without reading it.

✳ ✳ ✳

To the Royal Academy of Brusselles—

Gentlemen, I have perused your late mathematical Prize Question, proposed in lieu of one in Natural Philosophy, for the ensuing year, viz.:

"Une figure quelconque donnée, on demande d'y inscrire le plus grand nombre de fois possible une autre figure plus-petite quelconque, qui est aussi donnée." [Given any single figure, inscribe therein another smaller figure, which is also given, as many times as possible.]

I was glad to find by these following Words—

"l'Académie a jugé que cette découverte, en étendant les bornes de nos connoissances, ne seroit pas san utilité" [The academy has judged that this discovery, by widening the boundaries of our knowledge, will not be without utility]—

—that you esteem *Utility* an essential Point in your Enquiries, which has not always been the case with all Academies; and I conclude therefore that you have given this Question instead of a philosophical, or as the Learned express it, a physical one, because you could not at the time think of a physical one that promised greater *Utility.*

Permit me then humbly to propose one of that sort for your consideration, and through you, if you approve it, for the serious Enquiry of learned Physicians, Chemists, etc. of this enlightened Age.

It is universally well known, That in digesting our common Food, there is created or produced in the Bowels of human Creatures, a great Quantity of Wind.

That the permitting this Air to escape and mix with the Atmosphere, is usually offensive to the Company, from the fetid Smell that accompanies it.

That all well-bred People therefore, to avoid giving such Offence, forcibly restrain the Efforts of Nature to discharge that Wind.

That so retained contrary to Nature, it not only gives frequently great present Pain, but occasions future Diseases, such as habitual Cholics, Ruptures, Tympanies, &c., often destructive of the Constitution, & sometimes of Life itself.

Were it not for the odiously offensive Smell accompanying such Escapes, polite People would probably be under no more Restraint in discharging such Wind in Company, than they are in spitting, or in blowing their Noses.

My Prize Question therefore should be, *To discover some Drug wholesome and not disagreeable, to be mixed with our common Food, or Sauces, that shall render the Natural Discharges, of Wind from our Bodies, not only inoffensive, but agreeable as Perfumes.*

That this is not a chimerical Project, and altogether impossible, may appear from these Considerations. That we already have some Knowledge of Means capable of Varying that Smell. He that dines on stale Flesh, especially with much Addition of Onions, shall be able to afford a Stink that no Company can tolerate; while he that has lived for some Time on Vegetables only, shall have that Breath so pure as to be insensible to the most delicate Noses; and if he can manage so as to avoid the Report, he may any where give Vent to his Griefs, unnoticed. But as there are many to whom an entire Vegetable Diet would be inconvenient, and as a little Quick-Lime thrown into a Jakes will correct the amazing Quantity of fetid Air arising from the vast Mass of putrid Matter contained in such Places, and render it rather pleasing to the Smell, who knows but that a little Powder of Lime (or some other thing equivalent) taken in our Food, or perhaps a Glass of Limewater drank at Dinner, may have the same Effect on the Air produced in and issuing from our Bowels? This is worth the Experiment.

Certain it is also that we have the Power of changing by slight Means the Smell of another Discharge, that of our Water. A few Stems of Asparagus eaten, shall give our Urine a disagreeable Odour; and a Pill of Turpentine no bigger than a Pea, shall bestow on it the pleasing Smell of Violets. And why should it be thought more impossible in Nature, to find Means of making a Perfume of our *Wind* than of our *Water?*

For the Encouragement of this Enquiry (from the immortal Honour to be reasonably expected by the Inventor), let it be reasonably considered of how small Importance of Mankind, or to how small a Part of Mankind have been useful those Discoveries in Science that have heretofore made Philosophers famous. Are there twenty Men in Europe at this Day, the happier, or even the easier, for any Knowledge they have picked out of Aristotle? What Comfort can the Vortices of Descartes give to a Man who has Whirlwinds in his Bowels! The Knowledge of Newton's Mutual *Attraction* of the Particles of Matter, can it afford Ease to him who is racked by their mutual *Repulsion,* and the cruel Distensions it occasions? The Pleasure arising to a few Philosophers, from seeing, a few

Times in their Life, the Threads of Light untwisted, and separated by the Newtonian Prism into seven Colours, can it be compared with the Ease and Comfort every Man living might feel seven times a Day, by discharging freely the Wind from his Bowels? Especially if it be converted into a Perfume: For the Pleasures of one Sense being little inferior to those of another, instead of pleasing the *Sight* he might delight the *Smell* of those about him, & make Numbers happy, which to a benevolent Mind must afford infinite Satisfaction. The generous Soul, who now endeavours to find out whether the Friends he entertains like best Claret or Burgundy, Champagne or Madeira, would then enquire also whether they chose Musk or Lilly, Rose or Bergamot, and provide accordingly. And surely such a Liberty of *Ex-pressing* one's *Scenti-ments,* and *pleasing one another,* is of infinitely more Importance to human Happiness than that Liberty of the *Press,* or *of abusing one another,* which the English are so ready to fight & die for.

In short, this Invention, if compleated, would be, as *Bacon* expresses it, *bringing Philosophy home to Men's Business and Bosoms.* And I cannot but conclude, that in Comparison therewith, for *universal* and *continual* **Utility,** the Science of the Philosophers abovementioned, even with the Addition, Gentlemen, of your *"Figure quelconque"* and the Figures inscribed in it, are, all together, scarely worth a FART*hing.*

The Speech of Miss Polly Baker

1747

A Hoax That Was Widely Reprinted As Actual Fact

The Speech of Miss Polly Baker, before a Court of Judicature, at Connecticut near Boston in New-England; where she was prosecuted the Fifth Time, for having a Bastard Child: Which influenced the Court to dispense with her Punishment, and induced one of her Judges to marry her the next Day.

May it please the Honourable Bench to indulge me in a few Words: I am a poor unhappy Woman, who have no Money to fee Lawyers to plead for me, being hard put to it to get a tolerable Living. I shall not trouble your Honours with long Speeches; for I have not the Presumption to expect, that you may, by any Means, be prevailed on to deviate in your Sentence from the Law, in my Favour. All I humbly hope is, That your Honours would charitably move the Governor's Goodness on my Behalf, that my Fine may be remitted. This is the Fifth Time, Gentlemen, that I have been dragged before your Court on the same Account; twice I have paid heavy Fines, and twice have been brought to Publick

Punishment, for want of Money to pay those Fines. This may have been agreeable to the Laws, and I don't dispute it; but since Laws are sometimes unreasonable in themselves, and therefore repealed, and others bear too hard on the Subject in particular Circumstances; and therefore there is left a Power somewhat to dispense with the Execution of them; I take the Liberty to say, That I think this Law, by which I am punished, is both unreasonable in itself, and particularly severe with regard to me, who have always lived an inoffensive Life in the Neighbourhood where I was born, and defy my Enemies (if I have any) to say I ever wronged Man, Woman, or Child.

Abstracted from the Law, I cannot conceive (may it please your Honours) what the Nature of my Offence is. I have brought Five fine Children into the World, at the Risque of my Life; I have maintained them well by my own Industry, without burthening the Township, and would have done it better, if it had not been for the heavy Charges and Fines I have paid. Can it be a Crime (in the Nature of Things I mean) to add to the Number of the King's Subjects, in a new Country that really wants People? I own it, I should think it a Praise-worthy, rather than a punishable Action. I have debauched no other Woman's Husband, nor enticed any Youth; these Things I never was charged with, nor has any one the least Cause of Complaint against me, unless, perhaps, the Minister, or Justice, because I have had Children without being married, by which they have missed a Wedding Fee. But, can ever this be a Fault of mine?

I appeal to your Honours. You are pleased to allow I don't want Sense; but I must be stupified to the last Degree, not to prefer the Honourable State of Wedlock, to the Condition I have lived in. I always was, and still am willing to enter into it; and doubt not my behaving well in it, having all the Industry, Frugality, Fertility, and Skill in Economy, appertaining to a good Wife's Character. I defy any Person to say, I ever refused an Offer of that Sort: On the contrary, I readily consented to the only Proposal of Marriage that ever was made me, which was when I was a Virgin; but too easily confiding in the Person's Sincerity that made it, I unhappily lost my own Honour, by trusting to his; for he got me with Child, and then forsook me: That very Person you all know; he is now become a Magistrate of this Country; and I had Hopes he would have appeared this Day on the Bench, and have endeavoured to moderate the Court in my Favour; then I should have scorned to have mentioned it; but I must now complain of it, as unjust and unequal, That my Betrayer and Undoer, the first Cause of all my faults and Miscarriages (if they must be deemed such) should be advanced to Honour and Power in the Government, that punishes my Misfortunes with Stripes and Infamy.

I should be told, 'tis like, That were there no Act of Assembly in the Case, the Precepts of Religion are violated by my Transgressions. If mine, then, is a religious Offence, leave it to religious Punishments. You have already excluded me from the Comforts of your Church-Communion. Is not that sufficient? You believe I have offended Heaven, and must suffer eternal Fire: Will not that be sufficient? What Need is there, then, of your additional Fines and Whipping?

I own, I do not think as you do; for, if I thought what you call a Sin, was really such, I could not presumptuously commit it. But, how can it be believed, that Heaven is angry at my having Children, when to the little done by me towards it, God has been pleased to add his Divine Skill and admirable Workmanship in the Formation of their Bodies, and crowned it, by furnishing them with rational and im-mortal Souls. Forgive me, Gentlemen, if I talk a little extravagantly on these Matters; I am no Divine, but if you, Gentlemen, must be making Laws, do not turn natural and useful Actions into Crimes, by your Prohibitions. But take into your wise Consideration, the great and growing Number of Batchelors in the Country, many of whom from the mean Fear of the Expences of a Family, have never sincerely and honourably courted a Woman in their Lives; and by their Manner of Living, leave unproduced (which is little better than Murder) Hundreds of their Posterity to the Thousandth Generation. Is not this a greater Offence against the Publick Good, than mine? Compel them, then, by Law, either to Marriage, or to pay double the Fine of Fornication every Year.

What must poor young Women do, whom Custom have forbid to solicit the Men, and Who cannot force themselves upon Husbands, when the Laws take no Care to provide them any; and yet severely punish them if they do their Duty without them; the Duty of the first and great Command of Nature, and of Nature's God, *Encrease and Multiply.* A Duty, from the steady Performance of which, nothing has been able to deter me; but for its Sake, I have hazarded the Loss of the Publick Esteem, and have frequently endured Publick Disgrace and Punishment; and therefore ought, in my humble Opinion, instead of a Whipping, to have a Statue erected to my Memory.

Alice Addertongue
1732

I am a young Girl of about thirty-five, and live at present with my Mother. I have no Care upon my Head of getting a Living, and therefore find it my Duty as well as Inclination, to exercise my Talent at CENSURE, for the Good of my Country folks. There was, I am told, a certain generous Emperor, who if a Day had passed over his Head, in which he had conferred no Benefit on any Man, used to say to his Friends, in Latin, *Diem perdidi;* that is, it seems, *I have lost a Day.* I believe I should make use of the same Expression, if it were possible for a Day to pass in which I had not, or missed, an Opportunity to scandalize somebody: But, Thanks be praised, no such Misfortune has befell me these dozen Years.

Yet whatever Good I may do, I cannot pretend that I first entered into the Practice of this Virtue from a Principle of Publick Spirit; for I remember that when a Child, I had a violent Inclination to be ever talking in my own Praise, and being continually told that it was ill Manners, and once severely whipt for it, the confined Stream formed itself a new Channel, and I began to speak for the future in the Dispraise of others. This I found more agreeable to Company, and almost as much so to my self: For what great Difference can there be, between putting yourself up, or putting your Neighbour down? Scandal, like other Virtues, is in part its own Reward, as it gives us the Satisfaction of making ourselves appear better than others, or others no better than ourselves.

My Mother, good woman, and I, have heretofore differed upon this Account. She argued that Scandal spoilt all good Conversation, and I insisted that without it there could be no such Thing. Our Disputes once rose so high, that we parted Tea-Table, and I concluded to entertain my Acquaintance in the Kitchin. The first Day of this Separation we both drank Tea at the same Time but she with her visitors in the Parlor. She would not hear of the least Objection to any one's Character, but began a new sort of Discourse in some such queer philosophical Manner as this; *I am mightily pleased sometimes,* says she, *When I observe and consider that the World is not so bad as People out of humour imagine it to be. There is something amiable, some good Quality or other in every body. If we were only to speak of People that are least respected, there is* such a one *is very dutiful to her Father, and methinks has a fine Set of Teeth;* such a one *is very respectful to her husband;* such a one *is very kind to her poor neighbours, and besides has a very handsome Shape;* such a one *is always ready to serve a Friend, and in my Opinion there is not a Woman in Town that has a more agreeable Air and Gait.* This fine kind of Talk which lasted near half an Hour, she concluded by saying, *I do not doubt but every one of you have made the like Observations, and I should be glad to have the Conversation continued upon this Subject.* Just at that Juncture I peeped in at the Door, and never in my Life before saw such a Set of simple vacant Countenances; they looked somehow neither glad, nor sorry, nor angry, nor pleased, nor indifferent, nor attentive; but, (excuse the Simile) like so many blue wooden Images of rye Dough. I in the

Kitchin had already begun a ridiculous Story of Mr.——'s Intrigue with his Maid, and his Wife's Behaviour upon the Discovery; at some Passages we laughed heartily, and one of the gravest of Mama's Company, without making any Answer to her Discourse, got up *to go and see what the Girls were so merry about:* She was followed by a Second, and shortly after by a Third, till at last the old Gentlewoman found herself quite alone, and being convinced that her Project was impracticable, came her self and finished her Tea with us; ever since which *Saul also has been among the Prophets,* and our Disputes lie dormant.

By Industry and Application, I have made my self the Center of all the Scandal in the Province, there is little stirring but I hear of it. I began the World with this Maxim, *That no Trade can subsist without Returns,* and accordingly, whenever I received a good story, I endeavoured to give two or a better in the Room of it. My Punctuality in this Way of Dealing gave such Encouragement, that it has procured me an incredible deal of Business, which without Diligence and good Method it would be impossible for me to go through. For besides the Stock of Defamation thus naturally flowing in upon me, I practice an Art by which I can pump Scandal out of People that are the least enclined that way. Shall I discover my Secret? Yes; to let it die with me would be inhuman. If I have never heard ill of some Person, I always impute it to defective Intelligence; *for there are none without their Faults, no not one.* If she is a Woman, I take the first Opportunity to let all her Acquaintance know I have heard that one of the handsomest or best Men in Town has said something in Praise either of her Beauty, her Wit, her Virtue, or her good Management. If you know any thing of Humane Nature, you perceive that this naturally introduces a Conversation turning upon all her Failings, past, present, and to come. To the same purpose, and with the same Success, I cause every Man of Reputation to be praised before his Competitors in Love, Business, or Esteem on Account of any particular Qualification. Near the Times of *Election,* if I find it necessary, I commend every Candidate before some of the opposite Party, listening attentively to what is said of him in answer: (But Commendations in this latter Case are not always necessary, and should be used judiciously); of late Years I needed only observe what they said of one another freely; and having for the Help of Memory taken Account of all Informations and Accusations received, whoever peruses my Writings after my Death, may happen to think, that during a certain Term, the People of Pennsylvania chose into all their Offices of Honour and Trust, the veriest Knaves, Fools and Rascals in the whole Province. The Time of Election used to be a busy Time with me, but this Year, with Concern I speak it, People are grown so good natured, so intent upon mutual Feasting and friendly Entertainment, that I see no Prospect of much Employment from that Quarter.

I mentioned above, that without good Method I could not go thro' my Business: In my Father's Lifetime I had some Instruction in Accompts, which I now apply with Advantage to my own Affairs. I keep a regular Set of Books, and can tell at an Hour's Warning how it stands between me and the World. In my *Day book* I enter every Article of Defamation as it is transacted; for Scandals *received in,* I give Credit; and when I pay them out again, I make the Persons to whom they respectively relate *Debtor.* In *my Journal,* I add to each Story by Way of Improvement, such probable Circumstances as I think it will bear, and in my *Ledger* the whole is regularly posted.

I suppose the Reader already condemns me in his Heart, for this particular of *adding Circumstances;* but I justify that part of my Practice thus. 'Tis a Principle with me, that none ought to have a greater Share of Reputation than they really deserve; if they have, 'tis an Imposition upon the Publick: I know it is every one's Interest, and therefore believe they endeavour, to conceal *all* their Vices and Follies; and I hold, that those People are *extraordinary* foolish or careless who suffer a *Fourth* of their Failings to come to publick Knowledge: Taking then the common Prudence and Imprudence of Mankind in a Lump, I suppose none suffer above *one Fifth* to be discovered: Therefore when I hear of any Person's Misdoing, I think I keep within Bounds if in relating it I only make it three *times* worse than it is; and I reserve to my self the Privilege of charging them with one Fault in four, which, for aught I know, they may be entirely innocent of. You see there are but few so careful of doing Justice as myself; what Reason then have Mankind to complain of *Scandal?* In a general way, the worst that is said of us is only half what might be said, if all our Faults were seen.

But alas, two great Evils have lately befallen me at the same time; an extream Cold that I can scarce speak, and a most terrible Toothache that I dare hardly open my Mouth: For some Days past I have received ten Stories for one I have paid; and I am not able to balance my Accounts without your Assistance. I have long thought that if you would make your Paper a Vehicle of Scandal, you would double the Number of your Subscribers. I send you herewith Account of 4 Knavish *Tricks,* 2 crackt *Maidenheads, 5 Cuckoldoms, 3 drubbed Wives,* and *4 Henpecked Husbands,* all within this Fortnight; which you may, as Articles of News, deliver to the Publick; and if my Toothache continues, shall send you more; being, in the mean time, Your constant Reader,

ALICE ADDERTONGUE

On Choosing A Mistress
1745

My dear Friend,

I know of no Medicine fit to diminish the violent natural Inclinations you mention; and if I did, I think I should not communicate it to you. Marriage is the proper Remedy. It is the most natural State of Man, and therefore the State in which you are most likely to find solid Happiness. Your Reasons against entering into it at present, appear to me not well-founded. The circumstantial Advantages you have in View by postponing it, are not only uncertain, but they are small in comparison with that of the Thing itself, the being *married and settled*. It is the Man and Woman united that make the compleat human Being. Separate, she wants his Force of Body and Strength of Reason; he, her Softness, Sensibility and acute Discernment. Together they are more likely to succeed in the World. A single Man has not nearly the Value he would have in that State of Union. He is an incomplete Animal. He resembles the odd Half of a Pair of Scissors. If you get a prudent healthy Wife, your Industry in your Profession, with her good Economy, will be a Fortune sufficient.

But if you will not take this Counsel, and persist in thinking a Commerce with the Sex inevitable, then I repeat my former Advice, that in all your Amours you should *prefer old Women to young ones*. You call this a Paradox, and demand my Reasons. They are these:

1. Because they have more Knowledge of the World and their Minds are better stored with Observations, their Conversation is more improving and more lastingly agreeable.

2. Because when Women cease to be handsome, they study to be good. To maintain their Influence over Men, they supply the Diminution of Beauty by an Augmentation of Utility. They learn to do a 1000 Services small and great, and are the most tender and useful of all Friends when you are sick. Thus they continue amiable. And hence there is hardly such a thing to be found as an old Woman who is not a good Woman.

3. Because there is no hazard of Children, which irregularly produced may be attended with much Inconvenience.

4. Because through more Experience, they are more prudent and discreet in conducting an Intrigue to prevent Suspicion. The Commerce with them is therefore safer with regard to your Reputation. And with regard to theirs, if the Affair should happen to be known, considerate People might be rather inclined to excuse an old Woman who would kindly take care of a young Man, form his Manners by her good Counsels, and prevent his ruining his Health and Fortune among mercenary Prostitutes.

5. Because in every Animal that walks upright, the Deficiency of the Fluids that fill the Muscles appears first in the highest Part: The Face first grows lank and wrinkled; then the Neck; then the Breast and Arms; the lower Parts continuing to the last as plump as ever: So that covering all above with a Basket, and regarding only what is below the Girdle, it is impossible of two Women to know an old one from a young one. And as in the dark all Cats are grey, the Pleasure or corporal Enjoyment with an old Woman is at least equal, and frequently superior, every Knack being by Practice capable of improvement.

6. Because the Sin is less. The debauching a Virgin may be her Ruin, and make her for Life unhappy.

7. Because the Compunction is less. The having made a young Girl *miserable* may give you frequent bitter Reflections; none of which can attend the making an old Woman *happy*.

8th and Lastly. They are *so grateful!*

* * *

The Antediluvians Were All Very Sober

The Antediluvians were all very sober
For they had no Wine, and they brewed no October;
All wicked, bad Livers, on Mischief still thinking,
For there can't be good Living where there is not
    good Drinking,   *Derry down.*

'Twas honest old Noah first planted the Vine,
And mended his Morals by drinking its Wine;
He justly the drinking of Water decried;
For he knew that all Mankind, by drinking it, died.
                                    Derry down.

From this Piece of History plainly we find
That Water's good neither for Body or Mind;
That Virtue and Safety in Wine-bibbing's found
While all that drink Water deserve to be drowned.
                                    Derry down.

So For Safety and Honesty put the Glass round.

The Oath

Luke, on his dying Bed, embraced his Wife,
And begged one Favour: Swear, my dearest Life,
Swear, if you love me, never more to wed,
Nor take a second Husband to your Bed.

Anne dropt a Tear. You know, my dear, says she,
Your least Desires have still been Laws to me;
But from this Oath, I beg you'd me excuse;
For I'm already promised to John Hughes.

Firm Resolve

Some have learnt many Tricks of sly Evasion,
Instead of Truth they use Equivocation,
And eke it out with mental Reservation,
Which is to good Men an Abomination.

Our Smith of late most wonderfully swore,
That whilst he breathed he would drink no more;
But since, I know his Meaning, for I think
He meant he would not breathe whilst he did drink.

Poor Richard
On His Deafness

Deaf, giddy, helpless, left alone,
To all my Friends a Burthen grown,
No more I hear a great Church Bell,
Than if it rang out for my Knell:

At Thunder now no more I start,
Than at the whisp'ring of a Fart.
Nay, what's incredible, alack!
I hardly hear my Bridget's Clack.

Poor Richard
On Fate

My sickly Spouse, with many a Sigh
Once told me—Dicky, I shall die:
I grieved, but recollected straight,
'Twas bootless to contend with Fate:

So Resignation to Heaven's Will
Prepared me for succeeding Ill;
'Twas well it did; for, on my Life,
'Twas Heaven's Will to spare my Wife.

Who's The Ass?

Once on a Time it by Chance came to pass,
That a Man and his Son were leading an Ass.
Cries a Passerby, Neighbor, you're shrewdly put to't,
To lead an Ass empty, and trudge it on foot.
Nay, quoth the old Fellow, if Folk do so mind us
I'll e'en climb the Ass, and Boy mount behind us:
But as they jogged on, they were laughed at and hissed,
What, two booby Lubbers on one sorry Beast!
This is such a Figure as never was known;
'Tis a sign that the Ass is none of your own.
Then down gets the Boy, and walks by the Side,
Till another cries, What, you old Fool must you ride?
When you see the poor Child that's weakly and young
Forced through thick and thin to trudge it along.
Then down gets the Father, and up gets the Son;
If this cannot please them we ne'er shall have done.
They had not gone far, but a Woman cries out,
O you young graceless Imp, you'll be hanged, no doubt!
Must you ride an Ass, and your Father that's grey
E'en foot it, and pick out the best of his Way?
So now to please all they but one Trick lack,
And that was to carry the Ass pick-pack:
But when that was tried, it appeared such a Jest,
It occasioned more Laughter by half than the rest.
Thus he who'd please all, and their Good-liking gain,
Shows a deal of Good-Nature, but labors in vain.

The Complaint

A Farmer once made a complaint to a Judge,
My Bull, if it please you, Sir, owing a Grudge,
Belike to one of your good Worship's Cattle,
Has slain him out-right in a mortal Battle:
I'm sorry at heart because of the Action,
And want to know how must be made Satisfaction.

Why, you must give me your Bull, that's plain
Says the Judge, or pay me the Price of the Slain.
But I have mistaken the Case, Sir, says John,
The dead Bull I talk of, and please you, 's my own:
And yours is the Beast that the Mischief has done.
The Judge soon replies with a serious Face:
Say you so? Then this Accident alters the case.

Time to Learn

Says Roger to his Wife, my dear;
The strangest piece of News I hear!
A Law, 'tis said, will quickly pass,
To purge the matrimonial Class;
Cuckolds, if any such we have here
Must to a Man be thrown i' th' River.
She smiling cried, My dear, you seem
Surprized! *Pray, han't you learned to swim?*

A Striking Sundial
1757

*H*ow to make a Striking Sundial, by which not only a Man's own Family, but all his Neighbours for ten Miles round, may know what o'Clock it is, when the Sun shines, without seeing the Dial.

Choose an open Place in your Yard or Garden, on which the Sun may shine all Day without any Impediment from Trees or Buildings. On the Ground mark out your Hour Lines, as for a horizontal Dial, according to Art, taking Room enough for the Guns. On the Line for One o'Clock, place one Gun; on the Two o'Clock Line two Guns, and so of the rest. The Guns must all be charged with Powder, but Ball is unnecessary. Your Gnomon or Style must have twelve burning Glasses annexed to it, and be so placed as that the Sun shining through the Glasses, one after the other, shall cause the Focus or burning Spot to fall on the Hour Line of One for Example, at one a Clock, and there kindle a Train of Gunpowder that shall fire one Gun. At Two a Clock, a Focus shall fall on the Hour Line of Two, and kindle another Train that shall discharge two Guns successively; and so of the rest.

Note, There must be 78 Guns in all. Thirty-two Pounders will be best for this Use; but 18 Pounders may do, and will cost less, as well as use less Powder, for nine Pounds of Powder will do for one Charge of each eighteen Pounder, whereas the Thirty-two Pounders would require for each Gun 16 Pounds.

Note also, That the chief Expence will be the Powder, for the Cannon once bought, will, with Care, last 100 Years. Note moreover, That there will be a great Saving of Powder in cloudy Days.

Kind Reader, Methinks I hear thee say, *That it is indeed a good Thing to know how the Time passes, but this Kind of Dial, notwithstanding the mentioned Savings, would be very expensive; and the Cost greater than the Advantage.* Thou art wise, my Friend, to be so considerate beforehand; some Fools would not have found out so much, till they had made the Dial and tried it. Let all such learn that many a private and many a publick Project, are like this *Striking Dial,* great Cost for little Profit.

Poor Richard's Almanack

Editor's Note: Franklin wrote and published Poor Richard's Almanack from 1733 through 1758, when he turned it over to his partner, David Hall. He started each almanac with an introductory essay, the first three of which are reprinted here. It should be understood that Richard Saunders was a fictitious character—although Franklin borrowed his name from an English astrologer who had lived in the previous century—as was Titan Leeds and all other "philomaths" who were issuing almanacs. Announcing the death of his principal competitor is not only a good example of Franklin's wit and satire, but likewise of his business acumen, for his almanac quickly became the most successful one in Pennsylvania.

1733

Courteous Reader,

I might in this place attempt to gain thy Favour, by declaring that I write Almanacks with no other View than that of the publick Good; but in this I should not be sincere; and Men are now a-days too wise to be deceived by Pretences how specious soever. The plain Truth of the Matter is, I am excessive poor, and my Wife, good Woman, is, I tell her, excessive proud; she cannot bear, she says, to sit spinning in her Shift of Tow, while I do nothing but gaze at the Stars; and has threatened more than once to burn all my Books and Rattling-Traps (as she calls my Instruments) if I do not make some profitable Use of them for the good of my Family. The Printer has offered me some considerable share of the Profits, and I have thus begun to comply with my Dame's desire.

Indeed this Motive would have had Force enough to have made me publish an Almanack many Years since, had it not been overpowered by my Regard for my good Friend and Fellow-Student, Mr. *Titan Leeds,* whose Interest I was extreamly unwilling to hurt: But this Obstacle (I am far from speaking it with Pleasure) is soon to be removed, since inexorable Death, who was never known to respect Merit, has already prepared the mortal Dart, the fatal Sister has already extended her destroying Shears, and that ingenious Man must soon be taken from us. He dies, by my Calculation made at his Request, on *Oct.* 17. 1733. 3 ho. 29 m. *P.M.* at the very instant of the conjunction of the Sun and Mercury: By his own Calculation he will survive till the 26th of the same Month. This small difference between us we have disputed whenever we have met these 9 Years past; but at length he is inclinable to agree with my Judgment; Which of us is most exact, a little time will now determine. As therefore these Provinces may not longer expect to see any of his Performances after this year, I think my self free to take up the Task, and request a share of the publick Encouragement; which I am the more apt to hope for on this Account, that the Buyer of my Almanack may consider himself, not only as purchasing an useful Utensil, but as performing an Act of Charity, to his poor Friend and Servant,

Richard Saunders.

1734

Courteous Readers,

Your kind and charitable Assistance last Year, in purchasing so large an Impression of my Almanacks, has made my Circumstances much more easy in the World, and requires my grateful Acknowledgment. My Wife has been enabled to get a Pot of her own, and is no longer obliged to borrow one from a Neighbour; nor have we ever since been without something of our own to put in it. She has also got a pair of Shoes, two new Shifts, and a new warm Petticoat; and for my part, I have bought a second-hand Coat, so good, that I am now not ashamed to go to Town or be seen there. These Things have rendered her Temper so much more pacifick than it used to be, that I may say, I have slept more, and more quietly within this last Year, than in the three foregoing Years put together. Accept my hearty Thanks therefor, and my sincere Wishes for your Health and Prosperity.

In the Preface to my last Almanack, I foretold the Death of my dear old Friend and Fellow-Student, the learned and ingenious Mr. *Titan Leeds,* which was to be on the 17th of *October, 1733, 3* h. 29 m. P. M. at the very Instant of the conjunction of the Sun and Mercury. By his own Calculation he was to survive till the 26th of the same Month, and expire in the Time of the Eclipse, near 11 a clock, A.M. At which of these Times he died, or whether he be really yet dead, I cannot at this present Writing positively assure my Readers; forasmuch as a Disorder in my own Family demanded my Presence, and would not permit me as I had intended, to be with him in his last Moments, to receive his last Embrace, to close his Eyes, and do the Duty of a Friend in performing the last Offices to the Departed. Therefore it is that I cannot positively affirm whether he be dead or not; for the Stars only show to the Skilful, what will happen in the natural and universal Chain of Causes and Effects; but 'tis well known, that the Events which would otherwise certainly happen at certain Times in the Course of Nature, are sometimes set aside or postponed for wise and good Reasons, by the immediate particular Dispositions of Providence; which particular Dispositions the Stars can by no Means discover or foreshow. There is however, (and I cannot speak it without Sorrow) there is the strongest Probability that my dear Friend is *no more;* for there appears in his Name, as I am assured, an Almanack for the Year *1734,* in which I am treated in a very gross and unhandsome Manner; in which I am called *a false Predicter, an Ignorant, a conceited Scribler, a Fool, and a Lyar.* Mr. *Leeds* was too well bred to use any Man so indecently and so scurrilously, and moreover his Esteem and Affection for me was extraordinary. So that it is to be feared, that Pamphlet may be only a Contrivance of some body or other, who hopes perhaps to sell two or three Year's Almanacks still, by the sole Force and Virtue of Mr. *Leeds's* Name; but certainly, to put Words into the Mouth of a Gentleman and a Man of Letters, against his Friend, which the meanest and most scandalous of the People might be ashamed to utter even in a drunken Quarrel, is an unpardonable Injury to his Memory, and an Imposition upon the Publick.

Mr. *Leeds* was not only profoundly skilfill in the useful Science he professed, but he was a Man of *exemplary Sobriety, a* most *sincere Friend,* and an *exact Performer of his Word.* These valuable Qualifications, with many others, so much endeared him to me, that although it should be so, that, contrary to all Probability, contrary to my Prediction and his own, he might possibly be yet alive, yet my Loss of Honour as a Prognosticator, cannot afford me so much Mortification, as his Life, Health and Safety would give me Joy and Satisfaction. I am,

Courteous and kind Reader, your poor Friend and Servant,

R. SAUNDERS

1735

Courteous Reader,

This is the third Time of my appearing in print, hitherto very much to my own Satisfaction, and, I have reason to hope, to the Satisfaction of the Publick also; for the Publick is generous, and has been very charitable and good to me. I should be ungrateful then, if I did not take every Opportunity of expressing my Gratitude; for *ingratum si dixeris, omnia dixeris:* I therefore return the Publick my most humble and hearty Thanks.

Whatever may be the Musick of the Spheres, how great soever the Harmony of the Stars, 'tis certain there is no Harmony among the Stargazers; but they are perpetually growling and snarling at one another like strange Curs, or like some Men at their Wives: I had resolved to keep the Peace on my own part, and affront none of them; and I shall persist in that Resolution: But having received much Abuse from Titan Leeds deceased, (Titan Leeds when living would not have used me so!) I say, having received much Abuse from the Ghost of Titan Leeds, who pretends to be still living, and to write Almanacks in spight of me and my Predictions, I cannot help saying, that tho' I take it patiently, I take it very unkindly. And whatever he may pretend, 'tis undoubtedly true that he is really defunct and dead. First because the Stars are seldom disappointed, never but in the Case of wise Men, *Sapiens dominabitur astris,* and they fore-showed his Death at the Time I predicted it. Secondly, 'Twas requisite and necessary he should die punctually at that Time, for the Honour of Astrology, the Art professed both by him and his Father before him. Thirdly, 'Tis plain to every one that reads his two last Almanacks (for 1734 and 35) that they are not written with that *Life* his Performances used to be written with; the Wit is low and flat, the little Hints dull and spiritless, nothing smart in them but Hudibras's Verses against Astrology at the Heads of the Months in the last, which no Astrologer but a *dead one* would have inserted, and no Man *living* would or could write such Stuff as the rest. But lastly, I shall convince him from his own Words, that he is dead, *(ex ore suo conademnatus est)* for in his Preface to his Almanack for 1734, he says, "Saunders adds another GROSS FALSEHOOD in his Almanack, viz. that by my own Calculation I shall *survive* until the 26th of the said Month October 1733, which is as *untrue* as the former." Now if it be, as Leeds says, *untrue* and a gross *Falsehood* that he survived till the 26th of October 1733, then it is certainly *true* that he died *before* that Time: And if he died before that Time, he is dead now, to all Intents and Purposes, any thing he may say to the contrary notwithstanding. And at what Time before the 26th is it so likely he should die, as at the Time by me predicted, viz. the 17th of October aforesaid? But if some People will walk and be troublesome after Death, it may perhaps be born with a little, because it cannot well be avoided unless one would be at the Pains and Expence of laying them in the Red Sea; however, they should not presume too much upon the Liberty allowed them; I know Confinement must needs be mighty irksome to the free Spirit of an Astronomer, and I am too compassionate to proceed suddenly to Extremities with it; nevertheless, tho' I resolve with Reluctance, I shall not long defer, if it does not speedily learn to treat its living Friends with better Manners. I am, Courteous Reader, Your obliged Friend and Servant,

R. SAUNDERS

A Whimsical Cook

Poor Richard's Almanack, 1748

On the 19th of this Month (January), Anno 1493, was born the famous Astronomer Copernicus, to whom we owe the Invention, or rather the Revival (it being taught by Pythagoras near 2000 Years before) of that now generally received System of the World which bears his Name, and supposes the Sun in the Center, this Earth a Planet revolving round it in 365 Days, 6 Hours, &c. and that Day and Night are caused by the Turning of the Earth on its own Axis once round in 24 h. &c.

The Ptolomean System, which prevailed before Copernicus, supposed the Earth to be fixed, and that the Sun went round it daily. Mr. Whitson, a modern Astronomer, says, the Sun is 230,000 times bigger than the Earth, and 81 Millions of Miles distant from it: That vast Body must then have moved more than 480 Millions of Miles in 24 h. A prodigious Journey round this little Spot! How much more natural is Copernicus's Scheme! Ptolemy is compared to a whimsical Cook, who, instead of Turning his meat in Roasting, should fix That, and contrive to have his whole Fire, Kitchen and all, whirling continually round it.

The Stonecutter

The Pennsylvania Gazette, 1731

Friday Night last, a certain Stonecutter was, it seems, in
a fair way of dying the Death of a Nobleman; for being caught
Napping with another Man's Wife, the injured Husband took
the Advantage of his being fast asleep, and with a Knife began
very diligently to cut off his Head. But the Instrument not
being equal to the intended Operation, much struggling
prevented Success; and he was obliged to content himself for
the present with bestowing on the Aggressor a sound Drubbing. The Gap made in the Side of the Stonecutter's Neck,
tho' deep, is not thought dangerous; but some People admire,
that when the Person offended had so fair and suitable an
Opportunity, it did not enter into his Head to turn Stonecutter himself.

The Boo Bee

The Pennsylvania Gazette, 1731

Thursday last, a certain Printer ['tis not customary to give Names at length on these Occasions] walking carefully in clean Cloaths over some Barrels of Tar on Carpenter's Wharff, the head of one of them unluckily gave way, and let a Leg of him in above his Knee. Whether he was upon the Catch at that time, we cannot say, but 'tis certain he caught a *Tartar.* 'Twas observed he sprung out again right briskly, verifying the common Saying, *As nimble as a Bee in a Tarbarrel.* You must know there are several sorts of *Bees:* 'tis true he was no *Honey Bee,* nor yet a *Humble Bee,* but a *Boo bee* he may be allowed to be, namely *B.F.*

N.B. *We hope the Gentleman will excuse this Freedom.*

A Certain Constable

The Pennsylvania Gazette, 1731

Sure some unauspicious cross-grained Planet, in Opposition to Venus, presides over the Affairs of Love about this Time. For we hear, that on Tuesday last, a certain Constable having made an Agreement with a neighbouring Female, to *Watch* with her that Night; she promised to leave a Window open for him to come in at; but he going his Rounds in the dark, unluckily mistook the Window, and got into a Room where another Woman was in bed, and her Husband it seems lying on a Couch not far distant. The good Woman perceiving presently that it could not possibly be her Husband, made so much Disturbance as to wake the good Man; who finding somebody had got into his Place without his Leave, began to lay about him unmercifully; and 'twas thought, that had not our poor mistaken Galant, called out manfully for Help (as if he were commanding Assistance in the King's Name) and thereby raised the Family, he would have stood no more Chance for his Life between the Wife and Husband, than a captive Louse between two Thumb Nails.

Transporting Rattle-Snakes
1751

*B*y a Passage in one of your late Papers, I understand
that the Government at home will not suffer our mistaken
Assemblies to make any Law for preventing or discouraging
the Importation of Convicts from Great Britain, for this kind
Reason, *'That such Laws are against the Publick Utility, as they tend
to prevent the IMPROVEMENT and WELL PEOPLING of the
Colonies.'*

Such a tender parental Concern in our *Mother Country* for
the *Welfare* of her Children, calls aloud for the highest Returns of Gratitude and Duty. This every one must be sensible
of: But 'tis said, that in our present Circumstances it is absolutely impossible for us to make *such* as are adequate to the
Favour. I own it; but nevertheless let us do our Endeavour.
'Tis something to show a grateful Disposition.

In some of the uninhabited Parts of these Provinces,
there are Numbers of these venomous Reptiles we call rattle-
snakes; Felons-convict from the Beginning of the World:
These, whenever we meet with them, we put to Death, by
Virtue of an old Law, *Thou shalt bruise his Head.* But as this is
a sanguinary Law, and may seem too cruel; and as however

mischievous those Creatures are with us, they may possibly change their Natures, if they were to change the Climate; I would humbly propose, that this general Sentence of *Death* be changed for *Transportation.*

In the Spring of the Year, when they first creep out of their Holes, they are feeble, heavy, slow, and easily taken; and if a small Bounty were allowed *per* Head, some Thousands might be collected annually, and *transported* to Britain. There I would propose to have them carefully distributed in *St. James's Park,* in the *Spring-Gardens* and other Places of Pleasure about *London;* in the Gardens of all the Nobility and Gentry throughout the Nation; but particularly in the Gardens of the *Prime Ministers,* the *Lords of Trade* and *Members of Parliament;* for to them we are *most particularly* obliged.

There is no human Scheme so perfect, but some Inconveniencies may be objected to it: Yet when the Conveniencies far exceed, the Scheme is judged Operational, and fit to be executed. Thus Inconveniencies have been objected to that good and *wise* Act of Parliament, by virtue of which all the *Newgates* and *Dungeons* in *Britain* are emptied into the Colonies. It has been said, that these Thieves and Villains introduced among us, spoil the Morals of Youth in the Neighbourhoods that entertain them, and perpetrate many horrid Crimes: But let not *private Interests* obstruct publick *Utility.* Our *Mother* knows what is best for us. What is a little *Housebreaking, Shoplifting,* or *Highway Robbing;* what is a *Son* now and then *corrupted* and *hanged,* a Daughter *debauched* and *poxed,* a Wife *stabbed,* a Husband's *Throat cut,* or a Child's *Brains beat out* with an Axe, compared with this 'IMPROVEMENT and WELL PEOPLING of the Colonies'!

Thus it may perhaps be objected to my Scheme, that the *Rattle-Snake is* a mischievous Creature, and that his changing his Nature with the Clime is a mere Supposition, not yet confirmed by sufficient Facts. What then? Is not Example more prevalent than Precept? And may not the honest rough British Gentry, by a Familiarity with these Reptiles, learn to *creep,* and to *insinuate,* and to *slaver,* and to *wriggle* into Place (and perhaps to *poison* such as stand in their Way)—Qualities of no small Advantage to Courtiers! In comparison of which 'Improvement and *Publick Utility,'* what is a *Child* now and then killed by their venomous Bite—or even a favourite *Lap-Dog?*

I would only add, That this Exporting of Felons to the Colonies, may be considered as a *Trade,* as well as in the Light of a *Favour.* Now all Commerce implies *Returns:* Justice requires them: There can be no Trade without them. And Rattle-Snakes *seem the most suitable Returns* for the *Human Serpents* sent us by our *Mother* Country. In this, however, as in every other Branch of Trade, she will have the Advantage of us. She will reap *equal* Benefits without equal Risque of the inconveniencies and Dangers. For the *Rattle-Snake* gives Warning before he attempts his Mischief; which the Convict does not.

AMERICANUS.

Rules for Making Oneself
A Disagreeable Companion
1750

RULES, by *the Observation of which, a Man of Wit and Learning, may nonetheless make himself a* disagreeable *Companion.*

Your Business is to *shine;* therefore you must by all means prevent the shining of others, for their Brightness may make yours the less distinguished. To this End:

1. If possible engross the whole Discourse; and when other Matter fails, talk much of yourself, your Education, your Knowledge, your Circumstances, your Successes in Business, your Victories in Disputes, your own wise Sayings and Observations on particular Occasions, &c. &c. &c.

2. If when you are out of Breath, one of the Company should seize the Opportunity of saying something; watch his Words, and, if possible, find somewhat either in his Sentiment or Expression, immediately to contradict and raise a Dispute upon. Rather than fail, criticise even his Grammar.

3. If another should be saying an indisputably good Thing; either give no Attention to it; or interrupt him; or

draw away the Attention of others; or, if you can guess what he would be at, be quick and say it before him; or, if he gets it said, and you perceive the Company pleased with it, own it to be a good Thing, and withal remark that it had been said by *Bacon, Locke, Bayle,* or some other eminent Writer; thus you deprive him of the Reputation he might have gained by it, and gain some yourself, as you hereby show your great Reading and Memory.

4. When modest Men have been thus treated by you a few times, they will choose ever after to be silent in your Company; then you may shine on without Fear of a Rival; rallying them at the same time for their Dullness, which will be to you a new Fund of Wit.

Thus you will be sure to please *yourself.* The polite Man aims at pleasing *others,* but you shall go beyond him even in that. A Man can be present only in one Company, but may at the same time be absent in twenty. He can please only where he is, you wherever you are *not.*

Anthony Afterwit
1732

I am an honest Tradesman, who never meant Harm to any Body. My Affairs went on smoothly while a Batchelor; but of late I have met With some Difficulties, of which I take the Freedom to give you an Account.

About the Time I first addressed my present Spouse, her Father gave out in Speeches, that If she married a Man he liked, he would give with her £200 on the Day of Marriage. 'Tis true he never said so to me, but he always received me very kindly at his House, and openly countenanced my Courtship. I formed several fine Schemes, what to do with this same £200 and in some Measure neglected my Business on that Account: But unluckily it came to pass, that when the old Gentleman saw I was pretty well engaged, and that the Match was too far gone to be easily broke off; he, without any Reason given, grew very angry, forbid me the House, and told his Daughter that if she married me he would not give her a Farthing. However (as he foresaw) we were not to be disappointed in that Manner; but having stole a Wedding, I took her home to my House; where we were not in quite so poor a Condition as the Couple described in the Scotch Song, who had

> *Neither Pot nor Pan,*
> *But four bare Legs together;*

for I had a House tolerably furnished, for an ordinary Man, before. No thanks to Dad, who I understand was very much pleased with his politick Management. And I have since learned that there are old Curmudgeons *(so called)* besides him, who have this Trick, to marry their Daughters, and yet keep what they might well spare, till they can keep it no longer: But this by way of Digression; *A Word to the Wise is enough.*

    I soon saw that with Care and Industry we might live tolerably easy, and in Credit with our Neighbours: But my Wife had a strong Inclination to be a Gentlewoman. In Consequence of this, my old-fashioned Looking-Glass was one Day broke, as she said, *No Mortal could tell which way.* However, since we could not be without a Glass in the Room, *My Dear,* says she, *we may as well buy a large fashionable One that Mr. Such-a-one has to sell; it will cost but little more than a common Glass, and will be much handsomer and more creditable.* Accordingly the Glass was bought, and hung against the Wall: But in a Week's time, I was made sensible by little and little, *that the Table was by no Means suitable to such a Glass.* And a more proper Table being procured, My Spouse, who was an excellent Contriver, informed me where we might have very handsome Chairs *in the Way;* And thus, by Degrees, I found all my old Furniture stowed up into the Garret, and every thing below altered for the better.

    Had We stopped here, we might have done well enough; but my Wife being entertained with *Tea* by the Good

Women she visited, we could do no less than the like when they visited us; and so we got a *Tea-Table* with all its Appurtenances of *China* and *Silver*. Then my Spouse unfortunately overworked herself in washing the House, so that we could do no longer without a *Maid*. Besides this, it happened frequently, that when I came home at *One*, the Dinner was but just put in the Pot; for, *my Dear thought really it had been but Eleven:* At other Times when I came at the same Hour, *She wondered I would stay so long, for Dinner was ready and had waited for me these two hours*. These Irregularities, occasioned by mistaking the Time, convinced me, that it was absolutely necessary to *buy a Clock,* which my Spouse observed, *was a great Ornament to the Room!* And lastly, to my Grief, she was frequently troubled with some Ailment or other, and nothing did her so much Good as *Riding;* And *these Hackney Horses were such wretched ugly Creatures, that*—I bought a very fine pacing Mare, which cost £20. And hereabouts Affairs have stood for some Months past.

I could see all along, that this Way of Living was utterly inconsistent with my Circumstances, but had not Resolution enough to help it. Till lately, receiving a very severe Dun, which mentioned the next Court, I began in earnest to project Relief. Last Monday my Dear went over the River, to see a Relation, and stay a Fortnight, because *she could not bear the Heat of the Town*. In the Interim, I have taken my Turn to make Alterations, viz. I have turned away the Maid, Bag and Baggage (for what should we do with a Maid, who have (except my Boy) none but ourselves). I have sold the fine Pacing Mare, and bought a good Milch Cow, with £3 of the Money. I have disposed of the Tea Table, and put a Spinning Wheel in its Place, which methinks *looks very pretty:* Nine empty Canisters I have stuffed with Flax; and with some of the Money of the Tea-Furniture, I have bought a Set of Knitting-

Needles; for to tell you a Truth, which I would have go no farther, *I begin to want Stockings.* The stately Clock I have transformed into an Hour-Glass, by which I gained a good round Sum; and one of the Pieces of the old Looking-Glass squared and framed, supplies the Place of the Great One, which I have conveyed into a Closet, where it may possibly remain some Years. In short, the Face of Things is quite changed; and I am mightily pleased when I look at my Hour-Glass, *what an Ornament it is to the Room.* I have paid my Debts, and find Money in my Pocket. I expect my Dame home next Friday, and as your Paper is taken in at the House where she is, I hope the Reading of this will prepare her Mind for the above surprizing Revolutions. If she can conform to this new Scheme of Living, we shall be the happiest Couple perhaps in the Province, and, by the Blessing of God, may soon be in thriving Circumstances. I have reserved the great Glass, because I know her Heart is set upon it. I will allow her when she comes in, to be taken suddenly ill with the *Headach,* the *Stomach-ach, Fainting-Fits,* or whatever other Disorders she may think more proper; and she may retire to Bed as soon as she pleases: But if I do not find her in perfect Health both of Body and Mind the next Morning, away goes the aforesaid Great Glass, with several other Trinkets I have no Occasion for, to the Vendue that very Day. Which is the irrevocable Resolution of, Sir, Her loving Husband, and Your very humble Servant,

ANTHONY AFTERWIT

Postscript, You know we can return to our former Way of Living, when we please, if Dad will be at the Expence of it.

A Letter to his Sister, Jane
1758

*W*e have been together over a great part of England this Summer; and among other places visited the Town our Father was born in and found some Relations in that part of the Country still living. Our Cousin Jane Franklin, daughter of our Unkle John, died but about a Year ago. We saw her Husband Robert Page, who gave us some old Letters to his Wife from Unkle Benjamin. In one of them, dated Boston July 4, 1723 he writes "Your Unkle Josiah has a Daughter Jane about 12 years Old, a good humoured Child." So Jenny keep up your Character, and don't be angry when you have no Letters.

In a little Book he sent her, called *None but Christ,* he wrote an Acrostick on her Name, which for Namesakes' Sake, as well as the good Advice it contains, I transcribe and send you

> Illuminated from on High,
> And shining brightly in your Sphere
> Nere faint, but keep a steady Eye
> Expecting endless Pleasures there
> Flee Vice, as you'd a Serpent flee,
> Raise Faith and Hope three Stories higher
> And let Christ's endless Love to thee

Nere cease to make thy Love Aspire.
Kindness of Heart by Words express
Let your Obedience be sincere,
In Prayer and Praise your God Address
Nere cease 'till he can cease to hear.

After professing truly that I have a great Esteem and
Veneration for the pious Author, permit me a little to play
the Commentator and Critic on these Lines. The Meaning
of *Three Stories* higher seems somewhat obscure, you are to
understand, then, that *Faith, Hope* and *Charity* have been
called the three Steps of Jacob's Ladder, reaching from Earth
to Heaven. Our Author calls them *Stories,* likening Religion
to a Building, and those the three Stories of the Christian
Edifice; Thus Improvement in Religion, is called *Building Up,*
and *Edification. Faith is* then the Ground-floor, *Hope is up* one
Pair of Stairs. My dearly beloved Jenny, don't delight so
much to dwell in these lower Rooms, but get as fast as you
can into the Garret; for in truth the best Room in the House
is Charity. For my part, I wish the House was turn'd upside
down; 'tis so difficult (when one is fat) to get up Stairs; and
not only so, but I imagine *Hope* and *Faith* may be more firmly
built on *Charity, than Charity upon Faith* and *Hope.* However that
be, I think it a better reading to say

Raise Faith and Hope *one Story* higher.

Correct it boldly and I'll support the Alteration. For when
you are up two Stories already, if you raise your Building
three Stories higher, you will make five in all, which is two
more than there should be, you expose your upper Rooms
more to the Winds and Storms, and besides I am afraid the
Foundation will hardly bear them, unless indeed you build

with such light Stuff as Straw and Stubble, and that you know won't stand Fire.

Again where the Author Says

Kindness of Heart by Words express,

Strike out *Words* and put in *Deeds.* The world is too full of Compliments already; they are the rank Growth of every Soil, and Choak the good Plants of Benevolence and Benificence. Nor do I pretend to be the first in this comparison of Words and Actions to Plants; you may remember an Ancient Poet whose Words we have all Studied and Copied at School, said long ago,

A Man of Words and not of Deeds,
Is like a Garden full of Weeds.

'Tis pity that *Good Works* among some sorts of People are so little Valued, and *Good Words* admired in their Stead; I mean *seemingly pious Discourses* instead of *Humane Benevolent Actions.* These they almost put out of countenance, by calling Morality *rotten Morality,* Righteousness, *ragged Righteousness* and even *filthy Rags;* and when you mention *Virtue,* they pucker up their Noses as if they smelt a Stink; at the same time that they eagerly snuff up an empty canting Harangue, as if it was a Posie of the Choicest Flowers. So they have inverted the good old Verse, and say now

A Man of Deeds and not of Words
Is like a Garden full of _____.

I have forgot the Rhime, but remember 'tis something the very Reverse of a Perfume.

Father Abraham
Poor Richard, 1758

COURTEOUS READER,

I have heard that nothing gives an Author so great Pleasure, as to find his Works respectfully quoted by other learned Authors. This Pleasure I have seldom enjoyed; for tho' I have been, if I may say it without Vanity, an *eminent Author* of Almanacks annually now a full Quarter of a Century, my Brother Authors in the same Way, for what Reason I know not, have ever been very sparing in their Applauses; and no other Author has taken the least Notice of me, so that did not my Writings produce me some solid *Pudding,* the great Deficiency of *Praise* would have quite discouraged me.

I concluded at length, that the People were the best Judges of my Merit; for they buy my Works; and besides, in my Rambles, where I am not personally known, I have frequently heard one or other of my Adages repeated, with, *as Poor Richard says,* at the End on't; this gave me some Satisfaction, as it showed not only that my Instructions were regarded, but discovered likewise some Respect for my Authority; and I own, that to encourage the Practice of remembering and repeating those wise Sentences, I have sometimes *quoted myself with* great Gravity.

Judge then how much I must have been gratified by an Incident I am going to relate to you. I stopt my Horse lately where a great Number of People were collected at a Vendue of Merchant Goods. The Hour of Sale not being come, they were conversing on the Badness of the Times, and one of the Company called to a plain clean old Man, with white Locks, *Pray, Father* Abraham, *what think you of the Times? Won't these heavy Taxes quite ruin the Country? How shall we be ever able to pay them? What would you advise us to?*—Father *Abraham* stood up, and replied, If you'd have my Advice, I'll give it you in short, for a *Word to the Wise is enough, and many Words won't fill a Bushel,* as *Poor Richard* says. They joined in desiring him to speak his Mind, and gathering round him, he proceeded as follows;

Friends, says he, and Neighbours, the Taxes are indeed very heavy, and if those laid on by the Government were the only Ones we had to pay, we might more easily discharge them; but we have many others, and much more grievous to some of us. We are taxed twice as much by our *Idleness,* three times as much by our *Pride,* and four times as much by our *Folly,* and from these Taxes the Commissioners cannot ease or deliver us by allowing an Abatement. However let us hearken to good Advice, and something may be done for us; *God helps them that help themselves,* as *Poor Richard* says, in his Almanack of 1733.

It would be thought a hard Government that should tax its People one tenth Part of their *Time,* to be employed in its Service. But *Idleness* taxes many of us much more, if we reckon all that is spent in absolute *Sloth,* or doing of nothing, with that which is spent in idle Employments or Amusements, that amount to nothing. *Sloth,* by bringing on Diseases, absolutely shortens Life. *Sloth, like Rust, consumes faster than Labour wears, while the used Key is always bright,* as Poor *Richard* says. But *dost thou love Life, then do not squander Time, for that's the Stuff Life is made of,* as *Poor Richard* says.—How much more than is necessary do we spend in Sleep! forgetting that *The sleeping Fox catches no Poultry,* and that *there will be sleeping enough in the Grave,* as *Poor Richard* says. If Time be of all Things the most precious, wasting time must be, as *Poor Richard* says, *the greatest Prodigality, since, as* he elsewhere tells us, *Lost time is never found again;* and what we call *Time-enough, always proves little enough:* Let us then up and be doing, and doing to the Purpose; so by Diligence shall we do more with less perplexity. *Sloth makes all things difficult, but Industry all easy,* as *Poor Richard* says; and *He that riseth late, must trot all Day, and shall scarce overtake his Business at Night.* While *Laziness travels so slowly, that Poverty soon over takes him,* as we read in *Poor Richard,* who adds, *Drive thy Business, let not that drive thee;* and *Early to Bed, and early to rise, makes* a *Man healthy, wealthy and wise.*

So what signifies *wishing* and *hoping* for better Times. We may make these Times better if we bestir ourselves. *Industry need not wish,* as *Poor Richard* says, and *He that lives upon Hope will die farting. There are no Gains, without Pains; then Help Hands, for I have no Lands,* or if I have, they are smartly taxed. And, as *Poor Richard* likewise observes, *He that hath a Trade hath an Estate,* and *He that hath a Calling hath an Office of Profit and Honour;* but then the *Trade* must be worked at, and the *Calling* well followed, or neither the *Estate,* nor the *Office, will* enable us to pay our Taxes.—If we are industrious we shall never starve; for, as *Poor Richard* says, *At the working Man's House* Hunger *looks in, but dares not enter. Nor will the* Bailiff or the Constable enter, for *Industry pays Debts, while Despair encreaseth them,* says *Poor Richard.*—What though you have found no Treasure, nor has any rich Relation left you a Legacy, *Diligence is the Mother of Good-luck,* as *Poor Richard* says, and *God gives all Things to Industry. Then plough deep, while Sluggards sleep, and you shall have Corn to sell and to keep,* says *Poor Dick.* Work while it is called To-day, for you know not how much you may be hindered To-morrow, which makes *Poor Richard* say, *One To-day is worth two To-morrows;* and farther, *Have you somewhat to do to-morrow, do it To-day.* If you were a Servant, would you not be ashamed that a good Master should catch you idle? Are you then your own Master, *be ashamed to catch yourself idle,* as *Poor Dick* says. When there is so much to be done for yourself, your Family, your Country, and your gracious King, be up by Peep of Day; *Let not the Sun look down and say, Inglorious here he lies.* Handle your Tools without Mittens; remember that *the Cat in Gloves catches no Mice,* as *Poor Richard* says. 'Tis true there is much to be done, and perhaps you are weak handed, but stick to it steadily, and you will see great Effects, for constant *Dropping wears away Stones,* and by *Diligence and Patience the Mouse ate in two the Cable;* and *little Strokes fell great Oaks,* as *Poor Richard* says in his Almanack, the Year I cannot just now remember.

Methinks I hear some of you say, *Must a Man afford himself no Leisure?*—I will tell thee, my Friend, what *Poor Richard* says, *Employ thy Time well if thou meanest to gain Leisure;* and, *since thou art not sure of a Minute, throw not away an Hour.* Leisure, is Time for doing something useful; this Leisure the diligent Man will obtain, but the lazy Man never; so that, as *Poor Richard* says, *a Life of Leisure and a Life of Laziness are two Things.* Do you imagine that Sloth will afford you more Comfort than Labour? No, for as *Poor Richard* says, *Trouble springs from Idleness, and grievous Toil from needless Ease. Many without Labour, would live by their* WITS *only, but they break for want of Stock.* Whereas Industry gives Comfort, and Plenty, and Respect: *Fly Pleasures, and they will follow you. The diligent Spinner has a large shift;* and *now I have a Sheep and a Cow, every Body bids me Good morrow;* all which is well said by *Poor Richard.*

But with our Industry, we must likewise be *steady, settled* and careful, and oversee our own Affairs *with our own Eyes,* and not trust too much to others; for, as *Poor Richard* says,

> *I never saw an oft removed Tree,*
> *Nor yet an oft removed Family,*
> *That throve so well as those that settled be.*

And again, *Three Removes is as bad as a Fire;* and again, *Keep thy Shop, and thy Shop will keep thee;* and again, *If you would have your Business done, go; If not, send.* And again,

> *He that by the Plough would thrive,*
> *Himself must either hold or drive.*

And again, *The Eye of a Master will do more Work than both his Hands;* and again, *Want of Care does us more Damage than Want of Knowledge;* and again, *Not to oversee Workmen, is to leave them your Purse open.* Trusting too much to others Care is the Ruin of many; for, as the *Almanack* says, *In the Affairs of this World, Men are saved, not by Faith, but by the Want of it;* but a Man's own Care is profitable; for, saith *Poor Dick, Learning is to the Studious,* and *Riches to the Careful,* as well *as Power to the Bold,* and *Heaven to the Virtuous.* And farther, *If you would have a faithful Servant, and one that you like, serve yourself:* And again, he adviseth to Circumspection and Care, even in the smallest Matters, because sometimes *a little Neglect may breed great Mischief;* adding, *For want of a Nail the Shoe was lost; for want of a Shoe the Horse was lost; and for want of a Horse the Rider was lost,* being overtaken and slain by the Enemy, all for want of Care about a Horseshoe Nail.

So much for Industry, my Friends, and Attention to one's own Business; but to these we must add Frugality, if we would make our *Industry* more certainly successful. A Man may, if he knows not how to save as he gets, *keep his Nose all his life to the Grindstone, and* die not worth a *Groat* at last. *A fat Kitchen makes a lean Will,* as *Poor Richard* says; and,

> *Many Estates are spent in the Getting,*
> *Since Women for Tea forsook Spinning and Knitting,*

And Men for Punch forsook Hewing and Splitting.

If you would be wealthy, says he, in another Almanack, *think of Saving as well as of Getting:* The Indies *have not made* Spain *rich, because her* Outgoes *are greater than her* Incomes. Away then with your expensive Follies, and you will not have so much Cause to complain of hard Times, heavy Taxes, and chargeable Families; for, as *Poor Dick* says,

Women and Wine, Game and Deceit,
Make the Wealth small, and the Wants great.

And farther, *What maintains one Vice, would bring up two Children.* You may think perhaps, That a *little* Tea, or a *little* Punch now and then, Diet a *little* more costly, Clothes a *little* finer, and a *little* Entertainment now and then, can be no *great* Matter; but remember what *Poor Richard says, Many* a Little *makes a Mickle;* and farther, *Beware of* little *Expences; a small Leak will sink a great Ship;* and again, *Who Dainties love, shall Beggars prove;* and moreover, *Fools make Feasts, and wise Men eat them.*

Here you are all got together at this Vendue of *Fineries and Knicknacks.* You call them *Goods,* but if you do not take Care, they will prove *Evils* to some of you. You expect they will be sold *cheap,* and perhaps they may for less than they cost; but if you have no occasion for them, they must be *dear* to you. Remember what *Poor Richard* says, *Buy what thou hast no Need of and ere long thou shalt sell thy Necessaries.* And again, *At a great Pennyworth pause a while:* He means, that perhaps the Cheapness is *apparent* only, and not *real;* or the Bargain, by straitning thee in thy Business, may do thee more Harm than Good. For in another Place he says, *Many have been ruined by buying good Pennyworths.* Again, *Poor Richard* says, *'Tis foolish to lay out Money in a Purchase of Repentance; and* yet this Folly is prac-tised every day at Vendues, for want of minding *the Almanack. Wise Men,* as *Poor Dick* says, *learn by others Harms, Fools scarcely by their own;* but, *Felix quem faciunt aliena Pericula cautum.* Many a one, for the Sake of Finery on the Back, have gone with a hungry Belly, and half starved their Families; *Silks and Satins, Scarlet and Velvets,* as *Poor Richard* says, *put out the Kitchen Fire.* These are not the *Necessaries* of Life; they can scarcely be called the *Conveniencies,* and yet only because they look pretty, how many *want* to *have* them. The *artificial* Wants of Mankind thus become more numerous than the *natural;* and, as *Poor Dick* says, *For one* poor *Person, there are an hundred* indigent. By these, and other Extravagancies, the Genteel are reduced to Poverty, and forced to borrow of those whom they formerly despised, but who through *Industry* and *Frugality have maintained their* Standing; in which Case it appears plainly, that Plough-man *on his Legs is higher than a Gentleman on his Knees,* as *Poor Richard* says. Perhaps they have had a small Estate left them, which they knew not the Getting of; they think 'tis Day, *and will never be Night;* that a little to be spent out of so much, is not worth minding; *(a Child and a Fool,* as *Poor Richard* says, *imagine Twenty Shillings and Twenty years can never be spent)* but, *always taking out of the Meal-tub, and never putting in, soon comes to the Bottom;* then, as *Poor Dick* says, *When the Well's dry, they know the Worth of Water.* But this they might have known before, if they had taken his Advice; *If you would know the Value of Money, go and try to borrow some;* for, he that *goes a borrowing goes a sorrowing;* and indeed so does he that lends to such people, when he goes *to get it in again.*—*Poor Dick* farther advises, and says,

Fond Pride of Dress, *is sure a very Curse;*

E'er Fancy *you consult, consult your Purse.*

And again, *Pride is as loud a Beggar as Want, and a great deal more saucy.* When you have bought one fine Thing you must buy ten more, that your Appearance may be all of a Piece; but *Poor Dick* says, *'Tis easier to* suppress the *first Desire, than to* satisfy *all that follow it.* And 'tis as truly Folly for the Poor to ape the Rich, as for the Frog to swell, in order to equal the Ox.

> *Great Estates may venture more,*
> *But little Boats should keep near Shore.*

'Tis however a Folly soon punished; for *Pride that dines on Vanity sups on Contempt,* as *Poor Richard* says. And in another Place, *Pride breakfasted with Plenty, dined with Poverty, and supped with Infamy.* And after all, of what Use is this *Pride of Appearance, for which so much is* risked, so much is suffered? It cannot promote Health, or ease Pain; it makes no Increase of Merit in the Person, it creates Envy, it hastens Misfortune.

> *What is a Butterfly? At best*
> *He's but a Caterpillar drest.*
> *The Gaudy Fop's his Picture just,*

as *Poor Richard* says.

But what Madness must it be to run in *Debt for these* Superfluities! We are offered, by the Terms of this Vendue, *Six Months Credit;* and that perhaps has induced some of us to attend it, because we cannot spare the ready Money, and hope now to be fine without it. But, ah, think what you do when you run in Debt; *You give to another Power over your Liberty.* If you cannot pay at the Time, you will be ashamed to see your Creditor; you will be in Fear when you speak to him; you will make poor pitiful sneaking excuses, and by Degrees come to lose your Veracity, and sink into base downright lying; for, as *Poor Richard* says, *The second Vice is Lying, the first is running in Debt.* And again, to the same Purpose, *Lying rides upon Debt's Back.* Whereas a freeborn Englishman ought not to be ashamed or afraid to see or speak to any Man living. But Poverty often deprives a Man of all Spirit and Virtue: *'Tis hard for an empty Bag to stand upright,* as *Poor Richard* truly says. What would you think of that Prince, or that Government, who should issue an Edict forbidding you to dress like a Gentleman or a Gentlewoman, on Pain of Imprisonment or Servitude? Would you not say, that you are free, have a Right to dress as you please, and that such an Edict would be a Breach of your Privileges, and such a Government tyrannical? And yet you are about to put yourself under that Tyranny when you run in Debt for such Dress! Your Creditor has Authority at his Pleasure to deprive you of your Liberty, by confining you in Goal for Life, or to sell you for a Servant, if you should not be able to pay him! When you have got your Bargain, you may, perhaps, think little of Payment; but *Creditors, Poor Richard tells us, have better Memories than Debtors; and in* another Place says, *Creditors are a superstitious Sect, great Observers of set Days and Times.* The Day comes round before you are aware, and the Demand is made before you are prepared to satisfy it. Or if you bear your Debt in Mind, the term which at first seemed so long, will, as it lessens, appear extreamly short. Time will seem to have added Wings to his Heels as well as Shoulders. *Those have a short Lent,* saith *Poor Richard, who owe Money to be paid at Easter.* Then since, as he says, *The Borrower is a Slave to the Lender, and the Debtor to the Creditor,* disdain the Chain, preserve your Freedom; and maintain your Independency: Be *industrious* and *free;* be *frugal* and *free.* At present, perhaps, you may think yourself in thriving Circumstances, and that you can bear a little Extravagance without Injury; but,

> *For Age and Want, save while you may;*
> *No Morning Sun lasts a whole Day.*

as *Poor Richard* says.—Gain may be temporary and uncertain, but ever while you live, Expence is constant and certain; and *'tis easier to build two Chimnies than to keep one in Fuel,* as *Poor Richard* says. So *rather go to Bed supperless than rise in Debt.*

> *Get what you can, and what you get hold;*
> *'Tis the Stone that will turn all your Lead into Gold,*

as *Poor Richard* says. And when you have got the Philosopher's Stone, sure you will no longer complain of bad Times, or the

Difficulty of paying Taxes. This Doctrine, my Friends, is *Reason and Wisdom;* but after all, do not depend too much upon your own Industry, and Frugality, and *Prudence,* though excellent Things, for they may all be blasted without the Blessing of Heaven; and therefore ask that Blessing humbly, and be not uncharitable to those that at present seem to want it, but comfort and help them. Remember *Job* suffered, and was afterwards prosperous.

And now to conclude, *Experience keeps a dear School, but Fools will learn in no other, and scarce in that;* for it is true, *we may give Advice, but we cannot give Comfort,* as *Poor Richard* says: However, remember this, *They that won't be counselled, can't be helped,* as *Poor Richard* says. And farther, That *if you will not hear Reason, she'll surely rap your Knuckles.*

Thus the old Gentleman ended his Harangue. The People heard it, and approved the Doctrine, and immediately practised the contrary, just as if it had been a common Sermon; for the Vendue opened, and they began to buy extravagantly, notwithstanding all his Cautions, and their own Fear of Taxes.—I found the good Man had thoroughly studied my Almanacks, and digested all I had dropt on those Topicks during the Course of Five-and-twenty Years. The frequent Mention he made of me must have tired any one else, but my Vanity was wonderfully delighted with it, though I was conscious that not a tenth part of the Wisdom was my own which he ascribed to me, but rather the *Gleanings* I had made of the Sense of all Ages and Nations. However, I resolved to be the better for the Echo of it; and though I had at first determined to buy Stuff for a new Coat, I went away resolved to wear my old One a little longer. *Reader,* if thou wilt do the same, thy Profit will be as great as mine. *I am as ever,*
Thine to serve thee,
RICHARD SAUNDERS.

A Petition of the Left Hand
1785

TO THOSE WHO HAVE THE
SUPERINTENDENCY OF EDUCATION

I address myself to all the friends of youth, and conjure them to direct their compassionate regards to my unhappy fate, in order to remove the prejudices of which I am the victim. There are twin sisters of us; and the two eyes of man do not more resemble, nor are capable of being upon better terms with each other, than my sister and myself; were it not for the partiality of our parents, who make the most injurious distinctions between us. From my infancy, I have been led to consider my sister as a being of a more elevated rank. I was suffered to grow up without the least instruction, while nothing was spared in her education. She had masters to teach her writing, drawing, music, and other accomplishments; but if by chance I touched a pencil, a pen, or a needle, I was bitterly rebuked; and more than once I have been beaten for being awkward, and wanting a graceful manner. It is true, my sister associated me with her upon some occasions; but she always made a point of taking the lead, calling upon me only from necessity, or to figure by her side.

But conceive not, Sirs, that my complaints are instigated

merely by vanity. No; my uneasiness is occasioned by an object much more serious. It is the practice in our family, that the whole business of providing for its subsistence falls upon my sister and myself. If any indisposition should attack my sister—and I mention it in confidence upon this occasion, that she is subject to the gout, the rheumatism, and cramp, without making mention of other accidents—what would be the fate of our poor family? Must not the regret of our parents be excessive, at having placed so great a difference between sisters who are so perfectly equal? Alas! we must perish from distress; for it would not be in my power even to scrawl a suppliant petition for relief; having been obliged to employ the hand of another in transcribing the request which I have now the honour to prefer to you.

Condescend, Sirs, to make my parents sensible of the injustice of all exclusive tenderness, and of the necessity of distributing their care and affection among all their children equally. I am, with profound respect, Sirs, your obedient servant,

THE LEFT HAND.

The Mother Country
1765

We have an old Mother that peevish is grown,
She snubs us like Children that scarce walk alone;
She forgets we're grown up and have Sense of our own;
Which nobody can deny, deny, which nobody can deny.

If we don't obey Orders, whatever the Case;
She frowns, and she chides, and she loses all Pati-
Ence, and sometimes she hits us a Slap in the Face,
Which nobody can deny, &c.

Her Orders so odd are, we often suspect
That Age has impaired her sound Intellect:
But still an old Mother should have due Respect,
Which nobody can deny, &c.

Let's bear with her Humours as well as we can:
But why should we bear the Abuse of her Man?
When Servants make Mischief; they earn the Rattan,
Which nobody should deny, &c.

Know too, ye bad Neighbours, who aim to divide
The Sons from the Mother, that still she's our Pride;
And if ye attack her we're all of her side,
Which nobody can deny, &c.

We'll join in her Lawsuits, to baffle all those,
Who, to get what she has, will be often her Foes:
For we know it must all be our own, when she goes,
Which nobody can deny, deny, which nobody can deny.

The Frenchman and the Poker
1766

*I*t is reported, I know not with what Foundation, that there is an Intention of obliging the Americans to pay for all the Stamps they ought to have used, between the Commencement of the Act, and the Day on which the Repeal takes Place, *viz.* from the first of November 1765, to the first of *May* 1766; that this is to make Part of an Act, which is to give Validity to the Writings and Law Proceedings, that contrary to Law have been executed without Stamps, and is to be the Condition on which they are to receive that Validity. Shall we then keep up for a Trifle the Heats and Animosities that have been occasioned by the Stamp Act, and lose all the Benefit of Harmony and good Understanding between the different Parts of the Empire, which were expected from a generous total Repeal? Is this Pittance likely to be a Whit more easily collected than the whole Duty? Where are Officers to be found who will undertake to collect it? Who is to protect them while they are about it? In my Opinion, it will meet with the same Opposition, and be attended with the same Mischiefs that would have attended an Enforcement of the Act entire.

But I hear, that this is thought necessary, to raise a Fund for defraying the Expence that has been incurred by stamping so much Paper and Parchment for the Use of America, which they have refused to take and turned upon our Hands; and that since they are highly favoured by the Repeal, they cannot with any Face of Decency refuse to make good the Charges we have been at on their Account. The whole Proceeding would put one in Mind of the Frenchman that used to accost English and other Strangers on the *Pont-Neuf,* with many Compliments, and a red hot Iron in his Hand; *Pray Monsieur Anglois,* says he, *Do me the Favour to let me have the Honour of thrusting this hot Iron into your Backside?* Zoons, what does the Fellow mean! Begone with your Iron, or I'll break your Head! *Nay, Monsieur,* replies he, *if you do not choose it, I will not insist upon it. But at least, you will in Justice have the Goodness to pay me something for the heating of my Iron.*

Three Fables

NEW FABLES, humbly inscribed to the Secretary of State for the American Department.

I.

A Herd of Cows had long afforded Plenty of Milk, Butter, and Cheese to an avaricious Farmer, who grudged them the Grass they subsisted on, and at length mowed it to make Money of the Hay, leaving them to shift for Food as they could, and yet still expected to milk them as before; but the Cows, offended with his Unreasonableness, resolved for the future to suckle one another.

II.

An Eagle, King of Birds, sailing on His wings aloft over a Farmer's yard, saw a Cat there basking in the Sun, mistook it for a Rabbit, stooped, seized it, and carried it up into the Air, intending to prey on it. The Cat turning, set her Claws into the Eagle's Breast; who, finding his Mistake, opened his Talons, and would have let her drop; but Puss, unwilling to fall so far, held faster; and the Eagle, to get rid of the Inconvenience, found it necessary to set her down where he took her up.

A Lion's Whelp was put on board a Guinea Ship bound to America as a Present to a Friend in that Country: It was tame and harmless as a Kitten, and therefore not confined, but suffered to walk about the Ship at Pleasure. A stately, full-grown English Mastiff, belonging to the Captain, despising the Weakness of the young Lion, frequently took its Food by Force, and often turned it out of its Lodging Box, when he had a mind to repose therein himself. The Young Lion nevertheless grew daily in Size and Strength, and the Voyage being long, he became at last a more equal Match for the Mastiff; who continuing his Insults, received a stunning Blow from the Lion's Paw that fetched his Skin over his Ears, and deterred him from any future Contest with such growing Strength; regretting that he had not rather secured its Friendship than provoked its Enmity.

A cartoon designed and distributed by Franklin

A Letter to His Son, William
1773

I have written two pieces here lately for the Public
Advertiser, on American affairs, designed to expose the conduct of this country towards the colonies, in a short, compre-
hensive, and striking view, and stated therefore in out-of-the-
way forms, as most likely to take the general attention. The
first was called, *Rules by which a great empire may be reduced to a
small one;* the second, *An Edict of the king of Prussia.* I sent you
one of the first, but could not get enough of the second to
spare you one, though my clerk went the next morning to the
printer's, and wherever they were sold. They were all gone
but two. In my own mind I preferred the first, as a composi-
tion for the quantity and variety of the matter contained, and
a kind of spirited ending of each paragraph. But I find that
others here generally prefer the second. I am not suspected
as the author, except by one or two friends; and have heard
the latter spoken of in the highest terms as the keenest and
severest piece that has appeared here a long time. Lord
Mansfield I hear said of it, that it was *very* ABLE and *very*
ARTFUL indeed; and would do mischief by giving here a

bad impression of the measures of government; and in the colonies, by encouraging them in their contumacy. It is reprinted in the Chronicle, where you will see it, but stripped of all the capitalling and italicing, that intimate the allusions and marks the emphasis of written discourses, to bring them as near as possible to those spoken: printing such a piece all in one even small character, seems to me like repeating one of Whitfield's sermons in the monotony of a school-boy. What made it the more noticed here was, that people in reading it, were, as the phrase is, *taken in* till they had got half through it, and imagined it a real edict, to which mistake I suppose the king of Prussia's *character* must have contributed. I was down at lord Le Despencer's when the post brought that day's papers. Mr. Whitehead was there too (Paul Whitehead, the author of Manners) who runs early through all the papers, and tells the company what he finds remarkable. He had them in another room, and we were chatting in the breakfast parlour, when he came running into us, out of breath, with the paper in his hand. Here! says he, here's news for ye! *Here's the king of Prussia claiming a right to this kingdom!* All stared, and I as much as any body; and he went on to read it. When he had read two or three paragraphs, a gentleman present said, *Damn his impudence, I dare say we shall hear by next post that he is upon his march with one hundred thousand men to back this*. Whitehead who is very shrewd, soon after began to smoke it, and looking in my face said, *I'll be hanged if this is not some of your American Jokes upon us*. The reading went on, and ended with a abundance of laughing, and a general verdict that it was a fair hit: and the piece was cut out of the paper and preserved in my lord's collection.

Rules by Which A Great Empire May Be Reduced to a Small One

1773

An ancient Sage valued himself upon this, that tho' he could not fiddle, he knew how to make a *great City* of a *little one*. The Science that I, a modern Simpleton, am about to communicate is the very reverse.

I address myself to all Ministers who have the Management of extensive Dominions, which from their very Greatness are become troublesome to govern, because the Multiplicity of their Affairs leaves no Time *for fiddling*.

I. In the first Place, Gentlemen, you are to consider, that a great Empire, like a great Cake, is most easily diminished at the Edges. Turn your Attention therefore first to your remotest Provinces; that as you get rid of them, the next may follow in Order.

II. That the Possibility of this Separation may always exist, take special Care the Provinces are never incorporated with the Mother Country, that they do not enjoy the same common Rights, the same Privileges in Commerce, and that they are governed by *severer* Laws, all of *your enacting*, without allowing them any Share in the Choice of the Legislators. By carefully making and preserving such Distinctions, you will (to keep to my Simile of the Cake) act like a wise Gingerbread Baker, who, to facilitate a Division, cuts his Dough half through in those Places, where, when baked, he would have it *broken to Pieces.*

III. These remote Provinces have perhaps been acquired, purchased, or conquered, at the *sole Expence* of the Settlers or their Ancestors, without the Aid of the Mother Country. If this should happen to increase her *Strength* by their growing numbers ready to join in her Wars, her *Commerce* by their growing Demand for her Manufactures, or her *Naval Power* by greater Employment for her Ships and Seamen, they may probably suppose some Merit in this, and that it entitles them to some Favour; you are therefore to *forget it all,* or resent it as if they had done you Injury. If they happen to be zealous Whigs, Friends of Liberty, nurtured in Revolution Principles, *remember all that* to their Prejudice, and contrive to punish it: For such Principles, after a Revolution is thoroughly established, are of *no more Use,* they are even *odious* and *abominable.*

IV. However peaceably your Colonies have submitted to your Government, shewn their Affection to your Interest, and patiently borne their Grievances, you are to *suppose* them always inclined to revolt, and treat them accordingly. Quarter Troops among them, who by their Insolence may *provoke* the rising of Mobs, and by their Bullets and Bayonets *suppress* them. By this Means, like the Husband who uses his Wife ill *from Suspicion,* you may in Time convert your *Suspicions* into *Realities.*

V. Remote Provinces must have *Governors,* and *Judges,* to represent the Royal Person, and execute every where the delegated Parts of his Office and Authority. You Ministers know, that much of the Strength of Government depends on the *Opinion* of the People; and much of that Opinion on the

Choice of Rulers placed immediately over them. If you send them wise and good Men for Governors, who study the Interest of the Colonists, and advance their Prosperity, they will think their King wise and good, and that he wishes the Welfare of his Subjects. If you send them learned and upright Men for judges, they will think him a Lover of Justice. This may attach your Provinces more to his Government. You are therefore to be careful who you recommend for those Offices. If you can find Prodigals who have ruined their Fortunes, broken Gamesters or Stock-Jobbers, these may do well as Governors; for they will probably be rapacious, and provoke the People by their Extortions. Wrangling Proctors and pettyfogging Lawyers, too are not amiss, for they will be for ever disputing and quarrelling with their little Parliaments, if withal they should be ignorant, wrong-headed and insolent, so much the better. Attorneys Clerks and Newgate Solicitors will do for *Chief Justices,* especially if they hold their Places *during your Pleasure:* And all will contribute to impress those ideas of your Government that are proper for a People you *would wish to renounce it.*

VI. To confirm these Impressions, and strike them deeper, whenever the Injured come to the Capital with Complaints of Mal-administration, Oppression, or Injustice, punish such Suitors with long Delay, enormous Expence, and a final Judgment in Favour of the Oppressor. This will have an admirable Effect every Way. The Trouble of future Complaints will be prevented, and Governors and Judges will be encouraged to farther Acts of Oppression and Injustice; and thence the People may become more disaffected, *and at length desperate.*

VII. When such Governors have crammed their Coffers, and made themselves so odious to the People that they can no longer remain among them with Safety to their Persons, recall and *reward* them with Pensions. You may make them *Baronets* too, if that respectable Order should not think fit to resent it. All will contribute to encourage new Governors in the same Practices, and make the supreme Government *detestable.*

VIII. If when you are engaged in War, your Colonies should vie in liberal Aids of Men and Money against the common Enemy, upon your simple Requisition, and give far beyond their Abilities, reflect, that a Penny taken from them by your Power is more honourable to you than a Pound presented by their Benevolence. Despise therefore their voluntary Grants, and resolve to harrass them with novel Taxes. They will probably complain to your Parliaments that they are taxed by a Body in which they have no Representative, and that this is contrary to common Right. They will petition for Redress. Let the Parliaments flout their Claims, reject their Petitions, refuse even to suffer the reading of them, and treat the Petitioners with the utmost Contempt. Nothing can have a better Effect, in producing the Alienation proposed; for though many can forgive Injuries, *none ever forgave Contempt.*

IX. In laying these Taxes, never regard the heavy Burthens those remote People already undergo, in defending their own Frontiers, supporting their own provincial Governments, making new Roads, building Bridges, Churches and other public Edifices, which in old Countries have been done to your Hands by your Ancestors, but which occasion constant Calls and Demands on the Purses of a new People. Forget the *Restraints* you lay on their Trade for your *own* Benefit, and the Advantage a *Monopoly* of this Trade gives your exacting Merchants. Think nothing of the Wealth those Merchants and your Manufacturers acquire by the Colony Commerce; their encreased Ability thereby to pay Taxes at home; their accumulating, in the Price of their Commodities, most of those Taxes, and so levying them from their consuming Customers: All this, and the Employment and Support of thousands of your Poor by the Colonists, you are *intirely to forget.* But remember to make your arbitrary Tax more grievous to your Provinces, by public Declarations importing that your Power of taxing them has *no Limits,* so that when you take from them without their Consent a Shilling in the Pound, you have a clear Right to the other nineteen. This will probably weaken every Idea of *Security in their Property,* and convince them that under such a Government *they have nothing they can call their own;* which can scarce fail of producing *the happiest Consequences!*

X. Possibly indeed some of them might still comfort themselves, and say, "Though we have no Property, we have yet *something* left that is valuable; we have constitutional *Liberty* both of Person and of Conscience. This King, these Lords, and these Commons, who it seems are too remote from us to know us and feel for us, cannot take from us our *Habeas Corpus* Right, or our Right of Trial *by a Jury of our Neighbours:* They cannot deprive us of the Exercise of our Religion, alter our ecclesiastical Constitutions, and compel us to be Papists if they please, or Mahometans." To annihilate this Comfort, begin by Laws to perplex their Commerce with infinite Regulations impossible to be remembered and observed; ordain Seizures of their Property for every Failure; take away the Trial of such Property by Jury, and give it to arbitrary Judges of your own appointing, and of the lowest Characters in the Country, whose Salaries and Emoluments are to arise out of the Duties or Condemnations, and whose Appointments are *during Pleasure.* Then let there be a formal Declaration of both Houses, that Opposition to your Edicts is *Treason,* and that Persons suspected of Treason in the Provinces may, according to some obsolete Law, be seized and sent to the Metropolis of the Empire for Trial; and pass an Act that those there charged with certain other Offences shall be sent away in Chains from their Friends and Country to be tried in the same Manner for Felony. Then erect a new Court of Inquisition among them, accompanied by an armed Force, with Instructions to transport all such suspected Persons, to be ruined by the Expence if they bring over Evidences to prove their Innocence, or be found guilty and hanged if they can't afford it. And lest the People should think you cannot possibly go any farther, pass another solemn declaratory Act, that "King, Lords, and Commons had, hath, and of Right ought to have, full Power and Authority to make Statutes of sufficient Force and Validity to bind the unrepresented Provinces IN ALL CASES WHATSOEVER. This will include *Spiritual* with temporal; and taken together, must operate wonderfully to your Purpose, by convincing them, that they are at present under a Power something like that spoken of in the Scriptures, which can not only *kill their Bodies,* but *damn their Souls* to all Eternity, by compelling them, if it pleases, *to worship the Devil.*

XI. To make your Taxes more odious, and more likely to procure Resistance, send from the Capital a Board of Officers to superintend the Collection, composed of the most *indiscreet, ill-bred* and *insolent* you can find. Let these have large Salaries out of the extorted Revenue, and live in open grating Luxury upon the Sweat and Blood of the Industrious, whom they are to worry continually with groundless and expensive Prosecutions before the above-mentioned arbitrary Revenue-Judges, all *at the Cost of the Party prosecuted* tho' acquitted, because *the King is to pay no Costs.* Let these Men *by your Order* be exempted from all the common Taxes and Burthens of the Province, though they and their Property are protected by its Laws. If any Revenue Officers are *suspected* of the least Tenderness for the People, discard them. If others are justly complained of, protect and reward them. If any of the Under-officers behave so as to provoke the People to drub them, promote those to better Offices: This will encourage others to procure for themselves such profitable Drubbings, by multiplying and enlarging such Provocations, and *all will work to-wards the End you aim at.*

XII. Another Way to make your Tax odious, is to mis-apply the Produce of it. If it was originally appropriated for the *Defence* of the Provinces and the better Support of Gov-ernment, and the Administration of Justice where it may be *necessary,* then apply none of it to that *Defence,* but bestow it where it is *not necessary,* in augmented Salaries or Pensions to every Governor who has distinguished himself by his Enmity to the People, and by calumniating them to their Sovereign. This will make them pay it more unwillingly, and be more apt to quarrel with those that collect it, and those that im-posed it, who will quarrel again with them, and all shall con-tribute to your *main Purpose* of making them *weary of your Government.*

XIII. If the People of any Province have been accus-tomed to support their own Governors and Judges to Satis-faction, you are to apprehend that such Governors and Judges may be thereby influenced to treat the People kindly, and to do them Justice. This is another Reason for applying Part of that Revenue in larger Salaries to such Governors and Judges, given, as their Commissions are, *during your Pleasure* only, forbidding them to take any Salaries from their Pro-vinces; that thus the People may no longer hope any kindness from their Governors, or (in Crown Cases) any Justice from their Judges. And as the Money thus misapplied in one Pro-vince is extorted from all, probably *all will resent the Misappli-cation.*

XIV. If the Parliaments of your Provinces should dare to claim Rights or complain of your Administration, order them to be harassed with repeated *Dissolutions.* If the same Men are continually returned by new Elections, adjourn their Meetings to some Country Village where they cannot be accommodated, and there keep them *during Pleasure;* for this, you know, is your PREROGATIVE; and an excellent one it is, as you may manage it, to promote Discontents among the People, diminish their Respect, and *Increase their Disaffection.*

XV. Convert the brave honest Officers of your Navy into pimping Tide-waiters and Colony Officers of the Customs. Let those who in Time of War fought gallantly in Defence of the Commerce of their Countrymen, in Peace be taught to prey upon it. Let them learn to be corrupted by great and real Smugglers; but (to shew their Diligence) scour with armed Boats every Bay, Harbour, River, Creek, Cove or Nook throughout the Coast of your Colonies, stop and detain every Coaster, every Wood-boat, every Fisherman, tumble their Cargoes, and even their Ballast, inside out and upside down; and if a Penn'orth of Pins is found un-entered, let the Whole be seized and confiscated. Thus shall the Trade of your Colonists suffer more from their Friends in Time of Peace, than it did from their Enemies in War. Then let these Boats Crews land upon every Farm in their Way, rob the Orchards, steal the Pigs and Poultry, and insult the Inhabitants. If the injured and exasperated Farmers, unable to procure other Justice, should attack the Aggressors, drub them and burn their Boats, you are to call this *High Treason* and *Rebellion,* order Fleets and Armies into their Country, and threaten to carry all the Offenders three thousand Miles to be hanged, drawn and quartered. *O! this will work admirably!*

XVI. If you are told of Discontents in your Colonies,

never believe that they are general, or that you have given Occasion for them; therefore do not think of applying any Remedy, or of changing any offensive Measure. Redress no Grievance, lest they should be encouraged to demand the Redress of some other Grievance. Grant no Request that is just and reasonable, lest they should make another that is unreasonable. Take all your Informations of the State of the Colonies from your Governors and Officers in Enmity with them. Encourage and reward these *Leasing-makers;* secrete their lying Accusations lest they should be confuted; but act upon them as the clearest Evidence, and believe nothing you hear from the Friends of the People. Suppose all *their* Complaints to be invented and promoted by a few factious Demagogues, whom if you could catch and hang, all would be quiet. Catch and hang a few of them accordingly; and the *Blood of the Martyrs* shall *work Miracles* in favour of your Purpose.

XVII. If you see *rival Nations* rejoicing at the Prospect of your Disunion with your Provinces, and endeavouring to promote it: If they translate, publish and applaud all the Complaints of your discontented Colonists, at the same Time privately stimulating you to severer Measures; let not that *alarm* or offend you. Why should it? since you all mean *the same Thing.*

XVIII. If any Colony should at their own Charge erect a Fortress to secure their Port against the Fleets of a foreign Enemy, get your Governor to betray that Fortress into your Hands. Never think of paying what it cost the Country, for that would *look,* at least, like some Regard for Justice; but turn it into a Citadel to awe the Inhabitants and curb their Commerce. If they should have lodged in such Fortress the very Arms they bought and used to aid you in your Conquests, seize them all, 'twill provoke like *Ingratitude* added to *Robbery.*

One admirable Effect of these Operations will be, to discourage every other Colony from erecting such Defences, and so their and your Enemies may more easily invade them, to the great Disgrace of your Government, and of course *the Furtherance of your Project.*

XIX. Send Armies into their Country under Pretence of protecting the Inhabitants; but instead of garrisoning the Forts on their Frontiers with those Troops, to prevent Incursions, demolish those Forts, and order the Troops into the Heart of the Country, that the Savages may be encouraged to attack the Frontiers, and that the Troops may be protected by the Inhabitants: This will seem to proceed from your Ill will or your Ignorance, and contribute farther to produce and strengthen an Opinion among them, *that you are no longer fit to govern them.*

XX. Lastly, Invest the General of your Army in the Provinces with great and unconstitutional Powers, and free him from the Control of even your own Civil Governors. Let him have Troops enow under his Command, with all the Fortresses in his Possession; and who knows but (like some provincial Generals in the Roman Empire, and encouraged by the universal Discontent you have produced) he may take it into his Head to set up for himself. If he should, and you have carefully practised these few *excellent Rules* of mine, take my Word for it, all the Provinces will immediately join him, and you will that Day (if you have not done it sooner) get rid of the Trouble of governing them, and all the *Plagues* attending their *Commerce* and Connection from thenceforth and for ever.   Q.E.D.

An Edict of the King of Prussia
1773

Dantzick, September 5.

We have long wondered here at the Supineness of the English Nation, under the Prussian Impositions upon its Trade entering our Port. We did not till lately know the *Claims,* ancient and modern, that hang over that Nation, and therefore could not suspect that it might submit to those Impositions from a Sense of *Duty, or* from Principles of *Equity.* The following *Edict,* just made public, may, if serious, throw some Light upon this Matter.

FREDERICK, by the Grace of God, King of Prussia, &c. &c. &c. to all present and to come, HEALTH. The Peace now enjoyed throughout our Dominions, having afforded us Leisure to apply ourselves to the Regulation of Commerce, the Improvement of our Finances, and at the same Time the easing our *Domestic Subjects in* their Taxes: For these Causes, and other good Considerations us thereunto moving, We hereby make known, that after having deliberated these Affairs in our Council, present our dear Brothers, and other great Officers of the State, Members of the same, WE, of our certain Knowledge, full Power and Authority Royal, have made and issued this present Edict, viz.

WHEREAS it is well known to all the World, that the first German Settlements made in the Island of Britain, were by Colonies of People, Subjects to our renowned Ducal Ancestors, and drawn from *their* Dominions, under the Conduct of Hengist, Horsa, Hella, Uffa, Cerdicus, Ida, and others; and that the said Colonies have flourished under the Protection of our august House, for Ages past, have never been *emancipated* therefrom, and yet have hitherto yielded little Profit to the same. And whereas We Ourself have in the last War fought for and defended the said Colonies against the Power of France, and thereby enabled them to make Conquests from the said Power in America, for which we have not yet received adequate Compensation. And whereas it is just and expedient that a Revenue should be raised from the said Colonies in Britain towards our Indemnification; and that those who are Descendants of our ancient Subjects, and thence still owe us due Obedience, should contribute to the replenishing of our Royal Coffers, as they must have done had their Ancestors remained in the Territories now to us appertaining: WE do therefore hereby ordain and command, That from and after the Date of these Presents, there shall be levied and paid to our Officers of the Customs, on all Goods, Wares and Merchandizes, and on all Grain and other Produce of the Earth exported from the said Island of Britain, and on all Goods of whatever Kind imported into the same, a *Duty* of *Four and an Half* per Cent. *ad Valorem,* for the Use of us and our Successors.—And that the said Duty may more effectually be collected, We do hereby ordain, that all Ships or Vessels bound from Great Britain to any other Part of the World, or from any other Part of the World to Great Britain, shall in their respective Voyages touch at our Port of KONINGSBERG, there to be unladen, searched, and charged with the said Duties.

AND WHEREAS there have been from Time to Time discovered in the said Island of Great Britain by our Colonists there, many Mines or Beds of Iron Stone; and sundry Subjects of our ancient Dominion, skilful in converting the said Stone into Metal have in Times past transported themselves thither, carrying with them and communicating that Art; and the Inhabitants of the said Island, *presuming* that they had a natural Right to make the best Use they could of the natural Productions of their Country for their own Benefit, have not only built Furnaces for smelting the said Stone into Iron, but have erected Plating Forges, Slitting Mills, and Steel Furnaces, for the more convenient manufacturing of the same, thereby endangering a Diminution of the said Manufacture in our ancient Dominion. WE *do therefore* hereby farther ordain, that from and after the Date hereof, no Mill or other Engine for Slitting or Rolling of Iron, or any Plating Forge to work with a Tilt-Hammer, or any Furnace for making Steel, shall be erected or continued in the said Island of Great Britain: And the Lord Lieutenant of every County in the said Island is hereby commanded, on Information of any such Erection within his County, to order and by Force to cause the same to be abated and destroyed, as he shall answer the Neglect thereof to Us at his Peril. But We are nevertheless graciously pleased to permit the Inhabitants of the said Island to transport their Iron into Prussia, there to be manufactured, and to them returned, they paying our Prussian Subjects for the Workmanship, with all the Costs of Commission, Freight and Risque coming and returning, any Thing herein contained to the contrary notwithstanding.

WE do not however think fit to extend this our Indulgence to the Article of W*ool,* but meaning to encourage not only the manufacturing of woollen Cloth, but also the raising of Wool in our ancient Dominions, and to prevent *both,* as much as may be, in our said Island, We do hereby absolutely forbid the Transportation of Wool from thence even to the Mother Country Prussia; and that those Islanders may be farther and more effectually restrained in making any Advantage of their own Wool in the Way of Manufacture, We command that none shall be carried *out of one County into another,* nor shall any Worsted-Bay, or Woollen-Yarn, Cloth, Says, Bays, Kerseys, Serges, Frizes, Druggets, Cloth-Serges, Shalloons, or any other Drapery Stuffs, or Woollen Manufactures whatsoever, made up or mixt with Wool in any of the said Counties, be carried into any other County, or be Water borne even across the smallest River or Creek, on Penalty of Forfeiture of the same, together with the Boats, Carriages, Horses, &c. that shall be employed in removing them. *Nevertheless* Our loving Subjects there are hereby permitted, (if they think proper) to use all their Wool as *Manure for the Improvement of their Lands.*

AND WHEREAS the Art and Mystery of making *Hats* hath arrived at great Perfection in Prussia, and the making of Hats by our remote Subjects ought to be as much as possible restrained. And forasmuch as the Islanders beforementioned, being in Possession of Wool, Beaver, and other Furs, *have presumptuously* conceived *they* had a *Right to* make some Advantage thereof, by manufacturing the same into Hats, to the Prejudice of our domestic Manufacture, WE do therefore hereby strictly command and ordain, that no Hats or Felts whatsoever, dyed or undyed, finished or unfinished, shall be loaden or put into or upon any Vessel, Cart, Carriage or Horse, to be transported or conveyed *out of one County* in the said Island *into another County,* or to *any other Place whatsoever,* by any Person or Persons whatsoever, on Pain of forfeiting the same, with a Penalty of *Five Hundred Pounds* Sterling for every Offence. Nor shall any Hat-maker in any of the said Counties employ more than two Apprentices, on Penalty of *Five Pounds* Sterling per Month: We intending hereby that such Hat-makers, being so restrained both in the Production and Sale of their Commodity, may find no Advantage in continuing their Business. But lest the said Islanders should suffer Inconveniency by the Want of Hats, We are farther graciously pleased to permit them to send their Beaver Furs to *Prussia;* and We also permit Hats made thereof to be exported from *Prussia* to *Britain,* the People thus favoured to pay all Costs and Charges of Manufacturing, Interest, Commission to Our Merchants, Insurance and Freight going and returning, as in the Case of Iron.

And lastly, Being willing farther to favour Our said Colonies in *Britain,* We do hereby also ordain and command, that all the Thieves, Highway and Street-Robbers, House-breakers, Forgerers, Murderers, Sodomites, and Villains of every Denomination, who have forfeited their Lives to the Law in *Prussia,* but whom We, in Our great Clemency, do not think fit here to hang, shall be emptied out of our Gaols into the said Island of *Great Britain for the* BETTER PEOPLING of *that Country.*

We flatter Ourselves that these Our Royal Regulations and Commands will be thought *just* and *reasonable* by Our much-favoured Colonists in England, the said Regulations being copied from their own Statutes of 10 and 11 Will III. C. 10, 5 Geo. II. C 22.—23 Geo. II. C. 29.—4 Geo. I. C. II, and from other equitable Laws made by their Parliaments, or from Instructions given by their Princes, or from Resolutions of both Houses entered into for the GOOD *Government* of their own Colonies in Ireland and America.

And all Persons in the said Island are hereby cautioned not to oppose in any wise the Execution of this Our Edict, or any Part thereof, such Opposition being HIGH TREASON, of which all who are *suspected* shall be transported in Fetters from Britain to Prussia, there to be tried and executed according to the *Prussian* Law.

Such is our Pleasure.

Given at Potsdam this twenty-fifth Day of the Month of August, One Thousand Seven Hundred and Seventy-three, and in the Thirty-third Year of our Reign.

By the KING in his Council.

RECHTMAESSIG, *Secr.*

Some take this Edict to be merely one of the King's *Jeux d'Esprit:* Others suppose it serious, and that he means a Quarrel with England: But all here think the Assertion it concludes with, "that these Regulations are copied from *Acts* of the English Parliament respecting their Colonies," a very *injurious* one: it being impossible to believe, that a People distinguished for their *Love of Liberty,* a Nation so *wise, so liberal in its Sentiments, so just and equitable* towards its *Neighbours,* should, from mean and *injudicious* Views of *petty immediate Profit,* treat *its own Children* in a Manner so *arbitrary* and TYRANNICAL !

A Method of Humbling Rebellious American Vassals
1774

Sir—

Permit me, thro' the Channel of your Paper, to convey to the Premier, by him to be laid before his Mercenaries, our Constituents, my own Opinion, and that of many of my Brethren, Freeholders of this imperial Kingdom of the most feasible Method of humbling our rebellious Vassals of North America. As we have declared by our Representatives that we are the supreme Lords of their Persons and Property, and their occupying our Territory at such a remote Distance without a proper Control from us, except at a very great Expence, encourages a mutinous Disposition, and may, if not timely prevented, dispose them in perhaps less than a Century to deny our Authority, slip their Necks out of the Collar, and from being Slaves set up for Masters, more especially when it is considered that they are a robust, hardy People, encourage early Marriages, and their Women being amazingly prolific, they must of consequence in 100 Years be very numerous, and of course be able to set us at Defiance. Effectually to prevent which, as we have an undoubted Right to do, it is humbly proposed, and we do hereby give it as Part of our Instructions to our Representatives, that a Bill be brought in and passed, and Orders immediately transmitted to General Gage, our Commander in Chief in North America, in consequence of it, that all the Males there be castrated. He may make a Progress thro' the several Towns of North America at the Head of five Battalions, which we hear our experienced Generals, who have been consulted, think sufficient to subdue America if they were in open Rebellion; for who can resist the intrepid Sons of Britain, the Terror of France and Spain, and the Conquerors of America in Germany. Let a Company of Sow-gelders, consisting of 100 Men, accompany the Army. On their Arrival at any Town or Village, let Orders be given that on the blowing of the Horn all the Males be assembled in the Market Place. If the Corps are Men of Skill and Ability in their Profession, they will make great Dispatch, and retard but very little the Progress of the Army. There may be a Clause in the Bill to be left at the Discretion of the General, whose Powers ought to be very extensive, that the most notorious Offenders, such as Hancock, Adams, &c. who have been the Ringleaders in the Rebellion of our Servants, should be shaved quite close. But that none of the Offenders may escape in the Town of Boston, let all the Males there suffer the latter Operation, as it will be conformable to the modern Maxim that is now generally adopted by our worthy Constituents, that it is better that ten innocent Persons should suffer than that one guilty should escape. It is true, Blood will be shed, but probably not many Lives lost. Bleeding to a certain Degree is salutary. The English, whose Humanity is celebrated by all the World, but particularly by themselves, do not desire the Death of the Delinquent, but his Reformation. The Advantages arising from this Scheme being carried into Execution are obvious.

In the Course of fifty Years it is probable we shall not have one rebellious Subject in North America. This will be laying the Axe to the Root of the Tree. In the mean time a considerable Expence may be saved to the Managers of the Opera, and our Nobility and Gentry be entertained at a cheaper Rate by the fine Voices of our own Castrati, and the Specie remain in the Kingdom, which now, to an enormous Amount, is carried every Year to Italy. It might likewise be of Service to our Levant Trade, as we could supply the Grand Signor's Seraglio, and the Harams of the Grandees of the Turkish Dominions with Cargos of Eunuchs, as also with handsome Women, for which America is as famous as Circassia. I could enumerate many other Advantages. I shall mention but one: It would effectually put a Stop to the Emigrations from this Country now grown so very fashionable.

No Doubt you will esteem it expedient that this useful Project shall have an early Insertion, that no Time may be lost in carrying it into Execution. I am, Mr. Printer, (For myself, and in Behalf of a Number of independent Freeholders of Great Britain) Your humble Servant,

A FREEHOLDER OF OLD SARUM.

A Letter To A Friend in London
1774

Tell our good friend, Dr. Price, not to be in any pains for us, (because I remember he had his doubts) we are all firm and united. As I know he is a great calculator I will give him some data to work upon: ministry [England's colonial ministry] have made a campaign here, which has cost two millions, they have gained a mile of ground; they have lost half of it back again, they have lost fifteen hundred men, and killed one hundred and fifty Yankees. In the meantime we have had between sixty and seventy thousand children born. Ask him how long it will take for England to conquer America?

The King's Own Regulars
1775

Since you all will have singing, and won't be said, nay,
I cannot refuse where you so beg and pray;
So I'll sing you a song—as a body may say.
'Tis of the King's Regulars, who ne'er run way.
    O the old Soldiers of the King,
    and the King's own Regulars.

At Preston Pans we met with some Rebels one day,
We marshalled ourselves all in comely array:
Our hearts were all stout, and bid our legs stay,
But our feet were wrongheaded and took us away.
    O the old soldiers, &c.

At Falkirk we resolved to be braver,
And recover some credit by better behaviour;
We would not acknowledge feet had done us a favour;
So feet swore they would stand, but—legs ran however.
    O the old soldiers, &c.

No troops perform better than we at reviews;

We march and we wheel, and whatever you choose.
George would see how we fight, and we never refuse;
There we all fight with courage—
    you may see it in the news.
    O the old soldiers, &c.

To Monongahela with fifes and with drums
We marched in fine order, with cannon and bombs:
That great expedition cost infinite sums;
But a few irregulars cut us all into crumbs.
    O the old soldiers, &c.

It was not fair to shoot at us from behind trees:
If they had stood open as they ought before our great
    Guns we should have beat them with ease.
They may fight with one another that way if they please;
But it is not regular to stand and fight
    with such rascals as these.
    O the old soldiers, &c..

At Fort George and Oswego, to our great reputation,
We shewed our vast skill in fortification;
The French fired three guns, of the fourth they had no
    occasion;
For we gave up those forts, not thro' fear—but mere
    persuasion.
    O the old soldiers, &c.

To Ticonderoga we went in a passion,
Swearing to be revenged on the whole French nation.
But we soon turned tail, without hesitation
Because they fought behind trees which is not the fashion.
    O the old soldier, &c.

Grown proud at reviews, great George had no rest,
Each grandsire, he had heard a rebellion supprest.
He wished a rebellion, looked round and saw none,
So resolved a rebellion to make of his own—
    With the old soldiers, &c.

The Yankees he bravely pitched on,
    because he thought they would not fight,
And so he sent us over to take away their right,
But least they should spoil our review clothes, he cried
    braver and louder,
"For God's sake, brother kings, don't sell the cowards any
    powder."
    O the old soldiers, &c.

Our General with his council of war did advise,
How at Lexington we might the Yankees surprise.
We marched—and we marched—
    all surprised at being beat;
And so our wise General's plan of surprise was complete.
    O the old soldiers,&c.

For fifteen miles they followed and pelted us, we scarce
    had time to pull a trigger;
But did you ever know a retreat performed with more
    vigour?
For we did it in two hours which saved us from perdition,
'Twas not in *going out* but in *returning* consisted our
    expedition.
    O the old soldiers, &c.

Says our General, we were forced to take to our arms in
    our own defence:

(For *arms* read *legs,* and it will be both truth and sense.)
Lord Percy (says He) I must say something of him in
    civility,
And that is, I can never enough praise him for his
    great—agility.
    O the old soldiers, &c.

Of their firing from behind fences, he makes a great
    pother,
Every fence has two sides; they made use of one, and we
    only forgot to use the other.
That we turned our backs and ran away so fast,
    don't let that disgrace us;
'Twas only to make good what Sandwich said,
    "that the Yankees would not face us."
    O the old soldiers, &c.

As they could not get before us, how could they look us
    in the face?
We took care they should not, by scampering away
    apace;
That they had not much to brag of, is a very plain case.
For if they beat us in the fight, we beat them in the race.
    O the old soldiers of the King,
    and the King's own Regulars.

Petition of the Letter Z
1778

(Editor's Note: This short piece was written by Franklin as a way of venting his frustrations of dealing with Arthur Lee, who, along with Silas Deane, served with Franklin as America's commission to France at the beginning of the Revolutionary War. Isaac Bickerstaff was a pseudonym used by the satirst Jonathan Swift.)

To the Worshipful Isaac Bickerstaff, Esq.;
Censor-General
The Petition of the Letter Z, Commonly Called
Ezzard, Zed, or Izard, Most Humbly Sheweth,

He was always talking of his Family and of his being a Man of Fortune.

That your Petitioner is of as high extraction, and has as good an Estate as any other Letter of the Alphabet.

And complaining of his being treated, not with Respect

That there is therefore no reason why he should be treated with Disrespect and Indignity.

At the tail of the Commission, of Ministers

That he is not only placed at the Tail of the Alphabet, when he had as much **Right** as any other to be at the Head; but is, by the Injustice of his enemies totally excluded from the Word WISE, and his Place injuriously filled by a little, hissing, crooked, serpentine, venemous Letter called s, when it must be evident to your Worship, and to all the World, that Double U, I, S, E do not spell or sound *Wize*, but *Wice*.

He was not of the Commission for France, A Lee being preferred to him, which made him very angry; and the Char-acter here given of S, is just what he in his Passion gave Lee.

Your Petitioner therefore prays that the Alphabet may by your Censorial Authority be reformed, and that in Consideration of his *Long-suffering and Patience* he may be placed at the Head of it; that S may be turned out of the Word Wise, and the Petitioner employed instead of him;

The most impatient Man alive

And your Petitioner (as in Duty bound) shall ever pray, &c.

Z

Mr. Bickerstaff having examined the Allegations of the above Petition, judges and determines, that Z be admonished to be content with his Station, forbear Reflection upon his Brother Letters, & remember his own small Usefulness, and the little Occasion there is for him in the Republick of Letters, since S, whom he so despises, can so well serve instead of him.

The Grand Leap of the Whale
1765

Editor's Note: One of Franklin's favorite tricks was to write an article taking one point of view, then a week later, using a different pseudonym, submit a second article attacking the first one. That's just what he did in the following two pieces, both satirizing the tendency of the Press to exaggerate news accounts. Yet the tone of these two satires is gentle compared to the way he treats the press 25 years later, in the piece beginning on page 108.

✹ ✹ ✹

I have observed all the Newspapers have of late taken great Liberties with a noble Personage nearly allied to his Majesty. They have one Day made him Commander of a Fleet in the Mediterranean; again in the Channel; then to hoist his Flag on board a Yacht, and go on a grand Commission to Copenhagen; then to take a Tour to Brunswick, and so parade all over Germany to our unsatisfied Ally the King of Prussia; then he is said to commence Admiral again, and go with a large Fleet to America; first for a little Amusement to go a Cod Fishing With Monsieurs, and then to range the Continent, and I suppose they mean to go a Wood-hunting with the Cherokee Kings; these are the Peregrinations, that our noble Duke is to be sent upon; but indeed I am much surprised in all their high-flown Schemes they have never thought of sending him with a grand Squadron to East India up the Ganges to call upon the Nabob, and then advance and pay a Visit to the Great Mogul, and afterwards sail for China, and go up to see the Grandeur of the Court of Pekin: This would have been a fine Subject to have enlarged upon, and they might have thrown in how many sumptuous Barges were building to be sent on board the Squadron to be put together in India, and advance up the River with the utmost Magnificence. If these Hints will be any ways instructive to the Newswriters, I shall be happy to have pleased so useful a Body of Men in this great City.

THE SPECTATOR

✹ ✹ ✹

In your Paper of Wednesday last, an ingenious Correspondent that calls himself *the Spectator,* and dates from Pimlico, under the Guise of Good-Will to the News-Writers, whom he allows to be "an useful Body of Men in this great City," has, in my Opinion artfully attempted to turn them and their Works into Ridicule; wherein, if he could succeed, great Injury might be done to the Public, as well as to those good People.

Supposing, Sir, that the *We Hears* they give us of this and t'other intended Voyage, or Tour of this and t'other great Personage, were mere Inventions, yet they at least afford us an innocent Amusement while we read, and useful Matter of Conversation when we are disposed to converse. Englishmen, Sir, are too apt to be silent when they have nothing to say; too apt to be sullen when they are silent, and when they are sullen to hang themselves. But by these *We Hears* we are supplied with abundant Fund of Discourse: We discuss the Motives to such Voyages, the Probability of their being undertaken, and the Practicability of their Execution. Here we can display our Judgment in Politics, our Knowledge of the Interests of Princes, and our Skill in Geography; and (if we have it) shew our Dexterity moreover in Argumentation. In the mean time, the tedious Hours is killed; we go home pleased with the Applauses we have received from others, or at least with those we secretly give to ourselves; we sleep soundly, and live on, to the Comfort of our Families.

But, Sir, I beg leave to say, that all the Articles of News, that seem improbable, are not mere Inventions. Some of them, I can assure you on the Faith of a Traveller, are serious Truths. And here, quitting Mr. Spectator of Pimlico, give me Leave to instance the various numberless Accounts the News Writers have given us (with so much honest Zeal for the Welfare of Poor Old England!) of the establishing Manufactures in the Colonies to the Prejudice of those of this Kingdom. It is objected by superficial Readers, who yet pretend to some Knowledge of those Countries, that such Establishments are not only improbable but impossible; for that their Sheep have but little Wool, not in the whole sufficient for a Pair of Stockings a Year to each Inhabitants; and that, from the universal Dearness of Labour among them, the working of Iron and other Materials, except in some few coarse Instances, is impracticable to any Advantage. Dear Sir, do not let us suffer ourselves to be amused with such groundless Objections. The very Tails of the American Sheep are so laden with Wool, that each has a Car or Waggon on four little Wheels to support and keep it from trailing on the Ground. Would they caulk their Ships? would they fill their Beds? would they even litter their Horses with Wool if it was not both plenty and cheap? And what signifies Dearness of Labour, where an English Shilling passes for Five-and-twenty? Their engaging three hundred Silk Throwsters here in one Week for New York was treated as a Fable, because, forsooth, they have "no Silk there to throw." Those who made this Objection perhaps did not know, that at the same Time the Agents from the King of Spain were at Quebec contracting for 1000 Pieces of Cannon to be made there for the Fortifications of Mexico, with 25,000 Axes for their industrious Logwood-Cutters; and at New York engaging an annual Supply of warm Floor-Carpets for their West-India Houses; other Agents from the Emperor of China were at Boston in New-England treating about an Exchange of Raw-Silk for Wool, to be carried on in Chinese Jonks through the Straits of Magellan. And yet all this is as certainly true as the account, said to be from Quebec, in the Papers of last Week, that the Inhabitants of Canada are making Preparations for a Cod and Whale Fishery this Summer in the Upper Lakes. Ignorant People may object that the Upper Lakes are fresh, and that Cod and Whale are Salt-water Fish: But let them know, Sir, that Cod, like other Fish, when attacked by their Enemies, fly into any Water where they think they can be safest; that Whales, when they have a mind to eat Cod, pursue them wherever they fly; and that the grand Leap of the Whale in that Chase up the Fall of Niagara is esteemed by all who have seen it, as one of the finest Spectacles in Nature!

Really, Sir, the World is grown too incredulous: Pendulum like, it is ever swinging from one Extream to another. Formerly, every Thing printed was believed, because it was in Print: Now Things seem to be disbelieved for just the very same Reason. Wise Men wonder at the present Growth of Infidelity! They should have considered, when they taught People to doubt the Authority of Newspapers, and the Truth of Predictions in Almanacs, that the next Step might be a Disbelief in the well-vouched Accounts of Ghost and Witches, and Doubts even of the Truth of the Athanasian Creed.

Thus much I thought it necessary to say in favour of an honest Set of Writers, whose comfortable Living depends on collecting and supplying the Printers with News, at the small Price of Six-pence an Article; and who always show their Regard to Truth, by contradicting such as are wrong in a subsequent Article—for another Six-pence, to the great Satisfaction and Improvement of us Coffee-house Students in History and Politics, and the infinite Advantage of all future Livies, Rapins, Robertsons, Humes, Smollets, and Macaulays, who may be sincerely inclined to furnish the World with that *rara avis,* a true History.

A TRAVELLER

The Court of the Popular Press
1789

Editor's Note: Although himself a printer and publisher, Franklin was a sharp critic of the popular press, for reasons that are as valid today as they were 200 years ago. In this satire, he compares the press to an unofficial tribunal or court of law.

❋ ❋ ❋

POWER OF THIS COURT

It may receive and promulgate accusations of all kinds against all persons and characters among the citizens of the state, and even against all inferior courts; and may judge, sentence, and condemn to infamy, not only private individuals but public bodies, etc., with or without inquiry or hearing, *at the court's discretion.*

IN WHOSE FAVOR AND FOR WHOSE EMOLUMENT THIS COURT IS ESTABLISHED

It is in favor of about 1 citizen in 500, who, by education or practice in scribbling, has acquired a tolerable style as to grammar and construction so as to bear printing, or who is possessed of a press and a few types. This five-hundredth part of the citizens have the privilege of accusing and abusing the other 499 parts at their pleasure; or they may hire out their pens and press to others for that purpose.

PRACTICE OF THE COURT

It is not governed by any of the rules of common courts of law. The accused is allowed no grand jury to judge of the truth of the accusation before it is publicly made, nor is the name of the accuser made known to him, nor has he an opportunity of confronting the witnesses against him; for they are kept in the dark as in the Spanish court of Inquisition. Nor is there any petty jury of his peers sworn to try the truth of the charges. The proceedings are also some times so rapid that an honest, good citizen may find himself suddenly and unexpectedly accused; and in the same morning judged and condemned and sentence pronounced against him, that he is a rogue and a villain. Yet, if an officer of this court receives the slightest check for misconduct in this, his office, he claims immediately the rights of a free citizen by the Constitution and demands to know his accuser, to confront the witnesses, and to have a fair trial by a jury of his peers.

THE FOUNDATION OF ITS AUTHORITY

It is said to be founded on an article in the state constitution which establishes the *liberty of the press,* a liberty which every Pennsylvanian will fight and die for, though few of us, I believe, have distinct ideas of its nature and extent. It seems, indeed somewhat like the *liberty of the press that* felons have, by the common law of England, before conviction: that is, to be pressed to death or hanged. If by the *liberty of the press* were understood merely the liberty of discussing the propriety of public measures and political opinions, let us have as much of it as you please; but if it means the liberty of affronting, calumniating, and defaming one another, I, for my part, own myself willing to part with my share of it whenever our legislators shall please so to alter the law, and shall cheerfully consent to exchange my *liberty* of abusing others for the *privilege* of not being abused myself.

BY WHOM THIS COURT IS COMMISSIONED OR CONSTITUTED

It is not by any commission from the supreme executive council, who might previously judge of the abilities, integrity, knowledge, etc., of the persons to be appointed to this great trust, of deciding upon the characters and good fame of the citizens; for this court is above that council, and may *accuse, judge,* and *condemn it* at pleasure. Nor is it hereditary, as in the court of dernier resort in the peerage of England. But any man who can procure pen, ink, and paper, with a press, a few types, and a huge pair of *blacking* balls may commissionate himself; and his court is immediately established in the plenary possession and exercise of its rights. For if you make the least complaint of the judge's conduct, he daubs his blacking balls in your face wherever he meets you; and, besides tearing your private character to flitters, marks you out for the odium of the public, as an enemy to *the liberty of the press.*

OF THE NATURAL SUPPORT OF THESE COURTS

Their support is founded in the depravity of such minds as have not been mended by religion nor improved by good education:

There is a lust in man no charm can tame,
Of loudly publishing his neighbor's shame.

Hence,

> On eagle's wings immortal scandals fly,
> While virtuous actions are but born and die.
> —Dryden

Whoever feels pain in hearing a good character of his neighbor will feel a pleasure in the reverse. And of those who, despairing to rise into distinction by their virtues, are happy if others can be depressed to a level with themselves, there are a number sufficient in every great town to maintain one of these courts by their subscriptions. A shrewd observer once said that, in walking the streets in a slippery morning, one might see where the good-natured people lived by the ashes thrown on the ice before their doors; probably he would have formed a different conjecture of the temper of those whom he might find engaged in such a subscription.

OF THE CHECKS PROPER TO BE ESTABLISHED AGAINST THE ABUSE OF POWER IN THESE COURTS

Hitherto there are none. But since so much has been written and published on the federal Constitution, and the necessity of checks in all other parts of good government has been so clearly and learnedly explained, I find myself so far enlightened as to suspect some check may be proper in this part also. But I have been at a loss to imagine any that may not be construed an infringement of the sacred *liberty of the press*. At length, however, I think I have found one that, instead of diminishing general liberty, shall augment it; which is, by restoring to the people a species of liberty of which they have been deprived by our laws; mean the *liberty of the cudgel.*

In the rude state of society prior to the existence of laws, if one man gave another ill language, the affronted person would return it by a box on the ear and, if repeated, by a good drubbing; and this without offending against any law. But now the right of making such returns is denied, and they are punished as breaches of the peace; while the right of abusing seems to remain in full force, the laws made against it being rendered ineffectual by the *liberty of the press*.

My proposal, then, is to leave the *liberty of the press* untouched, to be exercised in its full extent, force, and vigor; but to permit the *liberty of the cudgel* to go with it *pari passu* [on equal footing]. Thus, my fellow citizens, if an impudent writer attacks your reputation, dearer to you perhaps than your life, and puts his name to the charge, you may go to him as openly and break his head. If he conceals himself behind the printer, and you can nevertheless discover who he is, you may in like manner waylay him in the night, attack him behind, and give him a good drubbing. Thus far goes my project as to private resentment and retribution. But if the public should ever happen to be affronted, as it ought to be with the conduct of such writers, I would not advise proceeding immediately to these extremities; but that we should in moderation content ourselves with tarring and feathering, and tossing them in a blanket.

If, however, it should be thought that this proposal of mine may disturb the public peace, I would then humbly recommend to our legislators to take up the consideration of both liberties, that of the press, and that of the cudgel, and by an explicit law mark their extent and limits; and, at the same time that they secure the person of a citizen from assaults, they would likewise provide for the security of his reputation.

The Encouragement of Idleness
1766

*T*o Messieurs the Public and Co.

I am one of that class of people that feeds you all, and at present is abused by you all; in short I am a *Farmer*.

By your News-papers we are told, that God had sent a very short harvest to some other countries of Europe. I thought this might be in favour to Old England; and that now we should get a good price for our grain, which would bring in millions among us, and make us flow in money, that to be sure is scarce enough.

But the wisdom of Government forbad the exportation.

Well says I, then we must be content with the market price at home.

No, says my Lords the mob, you shan't have that. Bring your corn to market if you dare; we'll sell it for you, for less money, or take it for nothing.

Being thus attacked by both ends *of the Constitution,* the head and the tail *of Government,* what am I to do? Must I keep my corn in barn to feed and increase the breed of rats? be it so; they cannot be less thankful than those I have been used to feed.

Are we Farmers the only people to be grudged the profits of honest labour? And why? One of the late scribblers against us gives a bill of fare of the provisions at my daughter's wedding, and proclaims to all the world that we had the insolence to eat beef and pudding! Has he never read that precept in the good book, *Thou shalt not muzzle the mouth of the ox that treadeth out the corn;* or does he think us less worthy of good living than our oxen?

O, but the Manufacturers! the Manufacturers! they are to be favoured, and they must have bread at a cheap rate!

Hark-ye, Mr. Oaf; The Farmers live splendidly, you say. And pray, would you have them hoard the money they get? Their fine cloaths and furniture, do they make them themselves, or for one another, and so keep the money among them? Or do they employ these your darling Manufacturers, and so scatter it again all over the nation?

My wool would produce me a better price if it were suffered to go to foreign markets. But that, Messieurs the Public, your laws will not permit. It must be kept all at home, that our *dear* Manufacturers may have it the cheaper. And then, having yourselves thus lessened our encouragement for raising sheep, you curse us for the scarcity of mutton!

I have heard my grandfather say, that the Farmers submitted to the prohibition on the exportation of wool, being made to expect and believe, that when the Manufacturer bought his wool cheaper, they should have their cloth cheaper. But the deuce a bit. It has been growing dearer and dearer from that day to this. How so? why truly the cloth is exported; and that keeps up the price.

Now if it be a good principle, that the exportation of a commodity is to be restrained, that so our own people at home may have it the cheaper, stick to that principle, and go thorough stitch with it. Prohibit the exportation of your cloth, your leather and shoes, your iron ware, and your manufactures of all sorts, to make them all cheaper at home. And cheap enough they will be, I'll warrant you—till people leave off making them.

Some folks seem to think they ought never to be easy, till England becomes another *Lubberland,* where 'tis fancied the streets are paved with penny rolls, the houses tiled with pancakes, and chickens ready roasted cry, come eat me.

I say, when you are sure you have got a good principle, stick to it, and carry it thorough. I hear 'tis said, that though it was *necessary and right* for the Ministry to advise a prohibition of the exportation of corn, yet it was *contrary to law;* and also, that though it was *contrary to law* for the mob to obstruct the waggons, yet it was *necessary and right.* Just the same thing, to a tittle. Now they tell me, an act of indemnity ought to pass in favour of the Ministry, to secure them from the consequences of having acted illegally. If so, pass another in favour of the mob. Others say, some of the mob ought to be hanged, by way of example. If so—but I say no more than I have said before, *when you are sure that you have got a good principle, go thorough with it.*

You say, poor labourers cannot afford to buy bread at a high price, unless they had higher wages. Possibly. But how shall we Farmers be able to afford our labourers higher wages, if you will not allow us to get, when we might have it, a higher price for our corn?

By all I can learn, we should at least have had a guinea a quarter more if the exportation had been allowed. And this money England would have got from foreigners.

But, it seems, we Farmers must take so much less, that the poor may have it so much cheaper.

This operates then as a tax for the maintenance of the poor. A very good thing, you will say. But I ask, Why a partial tax? Why laid on us Farmers only? If it be a good thing, pray, Messrs. the Public, take your share of it, by indemnifying us a little out of your public treasury. In doing a good thing there is both honour and pleasure; you are welcome to your part of both. For my own part, I am not so well satisfied of the goodness of this thing. I am for doing good to the poor, but I differ in opinion of the means. I think the best way of doing good to the poor, is not making them easy in poverty, but leading or driving them out of it. In my youth I travelled much, and I observed in different countries, that the more public provisions were made for the poor the less they provided for themselves, and of course became poorer. And, on the contrary, the less was done for them, the more they did for themselves, and became richer. There is no country in the world where so many provisions are established for them; so many hospitals to receive them when they are sick or lame, founded and maintained by voluntary charities; so many alms-houses for the aged of both sexes, together with a solemn general law made by the rich to subject their estates to a heavy tax for the support of the poor. Under all these obligations, are our poor modest, humble, and thankful; and do they use their best endeavours to maintain themselves, and lighten our shoulders of this burthen? On the contrary, I affirm that there is no country in the world in which the poor are more idle, dissolute, drunken, and insolent. The day you passed that act, you took away from before their eyes the greatest of all inducements to industry, frugality, and sobriety, by giving them a dependence on somewhat else than a careful accumulation during youth and health, for support in age or sickness. In short, you offered a premium for the encouragement of idleness, and you should not now wonder that it has had its effect in the increase of poverty. Repeal that law, and you will soon see a change in their manners.

St. Monday, and St. Tuesday, will cease to be holidays. *Six days shalt thou labour,* though one of the old commandments long treated as out of date, will again be looked upon as a respectable precept; industry will increase, and with it plenty among the lower people; their circumstances will mend, and more will be done for their happiness by inuring them to provide for themselves, than could be done by dividing all your estates among them.

Excuse me, Messrs. the Public, if upon this *interesting* subject, I put you to the trouble of reading a little of *my* nonsense. I am sure I have lately read a great deal of *yours;* and therefore from you (at least from those of you who are writers) I deserve a little indulgence.

ARATOR

The Dream

*H*aving completed the editing of this last piece, in which Franklin posed as the English farmer Arator, I sighed in relief, for it was to be the final piece of the collection. My work, at last, was done.

Giving myself leave to relax, therefore, I began to speculate on how Franklin would view a number of the conditions of modern American society, considering his forthright views on the idleness of poverty.

If Franklin foresaw the advent of St. Monday and St. Tuesday two hundred years ago, what would he say about celebrating our various public holidays on Mondays, so that the worker can get another cherished three-day weekend? Or about our system of civil service, which enshrines the largest bureaucracy on the face of the earth?

What would he say about day care? About medicare? About social security? About the plight of the homeless?

These speculations, and others like them, weighed so heavily on my brain, that my eyes became drowsy and my thought processes less frequent, until I fell fast asleep. And while asleep, I had a dream. It was, like Martin Luther King's, a dream of freedom. But it was not a dream of freedom to be won. It was a dream of freedom, once won, that has been given away.

In my dream, I imagined I was lifted up to heaven, where I was given a visitor's permit. Passing through the sacred portals, I was greeted by none other than Dr. Franklin himself.

"Your worries and fears have caught our attention," he said, by way of explanation. "Those of us whom you Modern Americans call the Founding Fathers are no less interested in the plight of our country today, in this place, than we were two hundred years ago. But we watch the years pass by with grave concern and sorrow.

"Two hundred years ago, we fought a war to establish freedom and liberty in these United States. But freedom and liberty are not land or gold—objects you can pass from generation to generation without depreciation or exhaustion. Freedom and liberty are intangible qualities. Once you have gained them, there are only two things you can do with them—preserve them by the utmost of vigilance and sacrifice, *or lose them!*

"The Modern American believes himself to be possessed of the great gift of freedom. But little does he know how little of the original gift is left. It is true that no foreign tyrant has invaded our fair shores and seized this precious gift from us. That has not been necessary. The Modern American has simply chosen the easier of the two options before him, *and has given his freedom away!*"

"To whom has he given this freedom?" I asked.

"To the government, of course," Franklin replied.

"But isn't the government of the people, for the people, and by the people?"

"In my time, it was. Even in the time of Abraham Lincoln, it was. But it is no more. You have given your freedoms and liberties away—not entirely, but to such a great extent that it is no longer anything but an exercise in nostalgia to say that America is a free country."

"I'm afraid I find this hard to believe," I protested.

"Then look at the evidence," Franklin replied. "In writing the Constitution that still governs this nation, we appended to that great document a set of 10 amendments called The Bill of Rights. These were written to guarantee that the government could not take from the states and citizens specific rights and freedoms. It did not, however, guarantee that the citizens, acting on their own, would not give to the government that which it was prohibited from taking. And this is what has happened.

"Look at the first Bill. 'Congress shall make no law respecting an establishment of religion or prohibiting the free exercise thereof, or abridging the freedom of speech or of the press, or the right of the people peaceably to assemble and to petition the government for a redress of grievances.'

"Modern Americans take great pride in this particular bill. But how much of it is left intact? In my day, we still had the freedom to utter a prayer at school, to start a session of Congress with an invocation, to erect a nativity scene on the courthouse lawn, and to read the Bible when we pleased. These rights have all been taken away by a pernicious doctrine called 'separation of Church and State.' Yet where does the original bill call for the separation of church and state? A nation which cannot pray together will soon have no ethics or moral standards. It will become a nation of opportunists, drunks, and drug users."

"I will grant you that. But surely we still have our freedom of speech and press?"

"Absolutely—if you call 'freedom' the ability to stand up and say innocuous things that everyone agrees with. But there is no honest dialogue in this country. Look at the furor that has arisen over the letters of H.L. Mencken. Here was one of the great editors, writers, and social critics of your century. But now he is being denounced as a bigot and racist because of a few isolated comments found by little-minded people in his letters. All of his many contributions to America are being vilified because of a few ruffled feathers—and the man is not even able to defend himself! And where are the editors of Modern America, the champions of free speech? Are they presenting a rational defense to this mischief? No— they are lighting the bonfire and helping the conflagration to spread! For shame, I say—shame! And you think you have a free press.

"The issue of free speech and a free press is not limited to what happens on television or in the papers, either. The tell-tale signs are more economic. Look at the taxes you suffer. Two hundred years ago, we fought a war to free ourselves from excessive taxation. In setting up the Constitution, one of the most important things we did was forbid the federal government from taxing the income of its citizens. This freedom was preserved for 150 years, until the citizens gave it away. And now look at how you are taxed!

"How can you believe that you are a free people when you willingly subject to an agency such as the Internal Revenue Service, which has the right to presume you are guilty until you prove yourself innocent! How can you believe you are a free people when you must spend days and weeks every year reporting your income to the government?

"In my day, the newspapers would be decrying these taxes as a vicious intrusion into our personal freedoms and self-expression. What do the newspapers and television stations of your day—the so-called champions of free speech—do? They run articles instructing the citizens on how to fill out their income tax forms! They have become the propaganda machines of the IRS.

"And when someone is hauled into tax court, does the media grasp the real issue? Do they raise their voices in protest against the excessive taxation of private capital in this country, and the tax laws that all but force citizens to break the law in order to obtain a ruling on what can be deducted and what cannot? No—they rake the citizen over the coals for social irresponsibility. Where is the free press? Where is free speech? It's a fairy tale.

"I will tell you one thing—if I were alive today, I would probably be spending most of my time in tax court, fighting to preserve whatever remaining scraps of freedom we have, before they were gone entirely. And Poor Richard would be raising hell about the rape of the American public by the Internal Revenue Service.

"You think there is still a great deal of freedom in our country? Look at the fourth Bill. It states that 'the right of the people to be secure in their persons, houses, papers, and effects against unreasonable searches and seizures shall not be violated, and no warrants shall issue, but upon probable cause, supported by oath or affirmation, and particularly describing the place to be searched and the persons or things to be seized.' "

"Many important court rulings have upheld this principle," I observed.

"Once again giving you the comfortable feeling of freedom, without the reality of it," Franklin replied. "The government and private agencies have compiled so many records on each citizen that there is no 'right to be secure in your own person, house, papers, and effects' in this modern age. Your phone calls can be traced—and even tapped—without your knowledge or consent. Everyone and his relatives demands to know your social security number, even though it is a direct invasion of your privacy. And with the advent of computers, all of these files can be checked and cross-checked in an instant.

"Let's look at the 7th Bill: 'In suits at common law, where the value in controversy shall exceed twenty dollars, the right of trial by jury shall be preserved, and no fact tried by a jury shall be otherwise reexamined in any court of the United States than according to the rules of the common law.'

"Here is a perfect example of the way Modern Americans have given away their freedom. The idea of trial by jury is based on 1) an educated electorate and 2) an electorate that recognizes the value of the jury system and willingly participates in it. The Modern American, however, so little values his or her freedom that, when called to serve on a jury, seeks to be excused from service, on the grounds of more pressing duties or activities.

"I devoted the last 40 years of my life to serving the cause of freedom in America; millions at that time and since have given their lives to preserve these freedoms and liberties. And yet, the Modern American is so ungrateful for these sacrifices that he is usually too busy to sit on a jury! As a result, there is no longer any such thing as a jury of one's peers—unless your peers happen to be uneducated, idle people who do not have anything better to do with their time!

"Freedom involves more than rights. For every right, there is a responsibility. None of the Bill of Rights can be sustained as a guardian of freedom and liberty unless each citizen is willing and able to do his or her share in acting with responsibility. When you fail to fulfill these responsibilities, you give away your rights—and your freedoms. Those who are lazy and irresponsible are unable to keep freedom.

"The frequency by which the first Bill of Rights is quoted makes me think, at times, that no one has bothered to read any further. When was the last time you read numbers 9 and 10? They state: 'The enumeration in the Constitution of certain rights shall not be construed to deny or disparage others retained by the people.' And: 'The powers not delegated to the United States by the Constitution, nor prohibited by it to the states, are reserved to the states respectively, or to the people.'

"What does this mean in plain English? It means that any power we did not specifically convey to the Congress cannot be assumed by them. The people must make a formal assignment of the power; it cannot be stolen from them in the dark of the night.

"In this regard, you can see the great danger of electing lawyers to serve in Congress. Having been trained to take any written statement and invert it so that it can be interpreted to mean the exact opposite of what is written, they have, over the years, found it convenient to forget to remind the citizens of this country that Congress can assume no power that is not specifically granted to it. And the good people of America have fallen into a deep sleep—deeper even than your own present condition—and allowed this sleight of hand to be perpetrated upon them.

"These are the reasons why I state that you have little left of the freedom America started with 200 years ago. The shells of freedom are still there, of course, but the substance has long ago been squandered. If I had to hazard a guess, I would say that only 20 percent of our original liberty remains, and perhaps only 10 percent of our freedom."

"That sounds awfully dire," I complained.

"Dire? Of course it's dire. Do you want the truth—or do you want the comfort of falsehoods and flattery? The truth of the matter, my dear friend, is that in Modern America, you do not any longer even have the freedom to fart!"

"I beg your pardon?"

"You see what I mean? You live in a sanitized society—a society that is so afraid of offending anyone that it is no longer possible to speak freely, a society that is so determined to prevent any kind of harm that it denies all liberty to everyone.

"If one toy out of a million manufactured chances to injure a child, that toy is immediately banned from production, even though 999,999 other children have found joy in playing with it.

"If one person out of ten million is offended by a joke or a comment made by a public official, that official is condemned and in all likelihood hounded out of public office, nothwithstanding all of the sacrifices and good works he or she may have performed over the years.

"If one person out of one hundred million is disturbed by the idea of capital punishment, then heaven forbid that we should use the gallows or the gas chamber, lest, that one individual should have indigestion, *and all the rest of us should be responsible for it!*

"This last spring, when a hurricane devastated the Carolinas, all you could hear on the news were people complaining about how long it took the government to take care of them. There was no debate as to whether it was the role of government to provide this relief, or whether they should accept it—just a blanket condemnation that it was slow in forthcoming.

"In my day, we held that the best government was the one that did as little as possible, leaving everything else to the citizens to do for themselves. Your modern day has reversed this philosophy, so that you believe that the best government is the one that does as much as possible, leaving little for the citizenry to do on their own.

"Please don't misunderstand me—I am as much in favor of disaster relief as anyone. But in my day, the citizens formed private societies to deal with these problems, so that the government would not be tempted to stick its nose where it didn't belong. I helped form fire companies, libraries, and relief societies, and not a one involved the government. So I know it can be done.

"You are welcome to your modern philosophy, although I would detest having to live by it. But you must realize that such a philosophy can only be implemented at the expense of freedom and liberty. In the land of the free and the home of the brave, the citizens govern themselves as much as possible. When they are no longer willing to do so, they trade in freedom and liberty for security and comfort. This is the fundamental difference between the America of 200 years ago and the America of today. And this is why I say you no longer have the freedom even to fart.

"In my day, we were not afraid to fart—or talk about it. We were not afraid to take risks, either. We did not envision a country where everyone was protected from every possible harm; quite the opposite, we envisioned a country where everyone had every possible chance to succeed. Somewhere along the way, I guess, we have lost the courage to fart.

"The Modern American cannot tolerate anything that is not squeaky clean, whether it is body odor, the smell of garbage, or language. You spend millions of dollars every year on deodorants, mouth rinses, and perfumes, so that you do not have to face the unpleasant smells of life. And if someone should happen to fart in your face, either literally or figuratively, you would run immediately for the nearest can of room deodorizer.

"This is how you handle the unpleasantries of life, as well. You mask them, so they will not offend you. But in doing so, you have given up your freedoms and liberties, and this ought to offend you. It stinks to high heaven, and I know whereof I speak, because high heaven happens to be my present home.

"For this reason, I am petitioning you, my good friend, to speak on my behalf. When you awaken from this dream, put down what I have said, and make it the final piece in your collection.

"Tell Modern America everything I have said, then add this *envoi* at the end:

"My brethren and countrymen, if you cherish freedom and liberty, you are going to have to learn to fart. You are going to have to get to the point where the comforts and securities of life are no longer sufficient exchange for your loss of freedom. Stop running to the government to protect you from every possible calamity. Take on the responsibilities of human living for yourself, and tell the government to get out of your life!

"The only tool of the average citizen—and it is a tremendous tool, when wielded with determination—is to take possession of your voice and start decrying the loss of freedom in this country. Write to your representatives and tell them that you want the government to give back the freedoms they have stolen from us. Write to the papers, and tell them that freedom of the press isn't worth a nickel unless it serves the people. Speak freely to your friends and colleagues, and awaken them to the loss of freedom in this nation.

"And when you are criticized, as you will be, remind your critics that you have the right to speak your mind. And if they shout you down, as they probably will, then inform them that since they insist on being asses, you will henceforth communicate with them with the appropriate part of your own anatomy. And turning to face them from the posterior, let them know where you stand. Let every fart count as a peal of thunder for liberty. Let every fart remind the nation of how much it has let pass out of its control.

"It is a small gesture, but one that can be very effective—especially in a large crowd. So fart, and if you must, fart often. But always fart without apology.

"Fart for freedom, fart for liberty—and fart proudly."